MW00604816

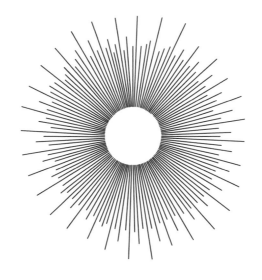

THE SCHOOL OF LOST BORDERS

A Love Story

Meredith Little Foster

Lost Borders Press

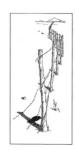

Lost Borders Press
P.O. Box 55
Big Pine, CA 93513
e-mail: lostbrdrs@cebridge.net
www.lostborderspress.com

Cover and book design by Sarah Underhill

First Edition
Manufactured in USA

I think Lost Borders will continue long after we are gone.
Its continuance will rely on those who see beyond gurus and personal longings
to who they are destined to be within the karmic consequences of their life.
Those visions mean nothing if they are not rooted to the reality of everyday life,
and to the sacred ancestors: We Who Have Gone Before.

The teachers of Lost Borders have come to help us in these times of greatest need.
They have been with us for many years,
not just because they deeply care about the work and the School,
but because they love us
as we love them.

– Steven Foster, 2000

*To the living, breathing, ancient pan-cultural
ceremony we call the Vision fast, that has guided, taught,
blessed, challenged, and brought back into balance the
heart blood of our humanity.*

*To all of nature, inside and out, that KNOWS how
to do this living and dying, and has so much to teach us,
if we would only listen.*

*And always, ALWAYS to Steven, to Ginnie,
and to our children, who sometimes had such great
patience for our obsession.*

Take Heart

By Selene Foster (age 10)

Stones spin
Feathers silence themselves
On the brisk air
In the space where you can hide
And take refuge from this harsh world
That we must live in
So take heart
Find a place where you can be free
To run, skip, play
To be a kid again
So that we may continue
On this road of living and dying

The School of Lost Borders

A Love Story

Part 3 – The School of Lost Borders

Part 4 – Breathing

Part 5 – Death is Sacred in All its Forms

Foreword

By Betsy Perluss

A story is not a story until it is told, given voice and the breath of life. Once it has been born, it flows like a river, downward with the passage of time. The story becomes geography, crafting the contours and canyons of our lives, and mapping the footprints of We Who Have Gone Before. Like a river in a hot desert, a good story nourishes life in an otherwise parched land. It seeps into our dry bones. It fills us up and gives us strength and vision to carry on. The story becomes our story as we share in the living waters.

This is such a story.

When I was first handed this book in its embryonic form, I could not put it down, reading late into the moon-filled night. At the time, I was in the Inyo Mountains of California, co-guiding the month-long training with the School of Lost Borders. All 18 of us involved in the training – participants and guides – were like a litter of jumping mice, sharing the same thirst, having heard time and time again the roaring of the Sacred River. This book took me right to the source, and I drank it up.

The conception of this book also took place in the Inyo Mountains, also during a month-long training. It was in 2012 when a participant asked Meredith if she would tell the story of how the School of Lost Borders came to be. Those who know Meredith know that she rarely talks about herself, especially her past. So when she paused before speaking those first words, "The story of the School is a love story," all ears tuned in with the realization that something extraordinary was about to take place.

A creation story was about to be told. And like most creation stories, this one included two very ordinary people, covered in the desert dust of humanity: an unreserved, rough-hewn older man with the wild look of coyote, and a shy, younger woman with compassion as big as the sea. Together, with the help of the gods, they would give birth to a movement we now call modern day rites of passage.

A love story, indeed.

It has been nearly 50 years since Steven and Meredith first met, and 15 years since Steven died. The river still runs strong and wild. Even in these hard rock times when borders seem to be rising in the most disturbing places – on our lands and in the hearts of many of its people – the river flows right on through, dissolving obstructions along its path. There is enough water for anyone who cares to take and drink, because it is our story, too. It is one of the millions that feed the sea of memory and creation.

This book is a testament to just how much we need such stories to survive. They are not for amusement or entertainment, although they are that, too. They are life.

This forward would not be complete without mentioning Joseph Lazenka who, in the wake of Steven's death, and 16 years thereafter, took the seat of director of the School of Lost Borders. It was Joseph's vision to put Meredith's story into book form. And I don't think it is a coincidence that in the same year of this book's publication, Joseph let go his title as director, stepping a little closer to the river, feeding the story, and edging onto the path of We Who Have Gone Before.

The School of Lost Borders is no longer made of Steven and Meredith, or Joseph, or any other singular person. It is made of many, spreading its influence across the globe. And even if one day the School ceases to exist, we can rest assured that the story will continue. It is in the geology of the land, imprinted on our hearts.

Introduction

This story is my story. I would only wish that it had the voice of Steven interwoven, as that's how we created and lived the WE story that always felt bigger than one of us or the other. Certainly his voice is in each of his books, both published and unpublished, and in the many people who still feel him close.

I miss that voice. I remember late-night talks with Ginnie many years ago about death. Steven said that he wanted to die before me, and I said that I wanted to take our passion to the end for both of us.

And so I have tried. I miss the WE voice that had such possibilities. Yet, I recognize that the WE is now the community of amazing people who have taken their place in the fabric of the School, dreaming into the future together as they listen to the needs of the people who come through in these challenging times.

The WE voice has grown to a roar.

So I offer the memories of a woman who met her love and together created something bigger than either of them – a form to carry this extraordinary ceremony, and profound teachings of the land, back into the homes and hearts of people from many cultures and many lands. Certainly, we were not the only ones to keep this ceremony alive. This is our story.

Acknowledgments

I must first acknowledge Joseph Lazenka, Petra Lentz-Snow, and Betsy Perluss, who urged and encouraged me to take this project on. Really, it was for love of them that I committed myself to doing this as best as I was able. To have Betsy right there, helping to shape it into its final form, has been invaluable. This is for them, and for the story that continues out in front of us.

It was Silke Schulze-Gattermann, a dear and respected friend from Germany, who then made all of this possible. She came for a week in the winter of 2016, and we sat every day for hours as she asked questions, encouraged me to talk from memory, and recorded our conversations. Somehow, miraculously, she took it all home and put it together into a readable manuscript. She has a gift and such a big heart. We are all grateful for her integrity, understanding, and smile.

I want to thank Gigi Coyle, Joseph, Petra and Emerald North, who live here in the Valley, or agreed to a Skype call, and gathered for council with Silke to give their perspective on the "early story." They brought many memories and insights that I didn't have.

We are also so grateful for Susan Hagen, a writer who took the early version of the manuscript and asked the questions that have made it more whole. She brought both her gifted professionalism and her insightful soul to turn this into a more readable book.

And thank you to each of my dear friends and colleagues who are the School, each with a piece of the vision in his or her homes and hearts. They represent "my people" – those who have walked with me, taught me, cared, and cherished the ceremony as much as Steven and I have. Without them, the School would certainly no longer exist.

And finally, I want to acknowledge the people who continued to believe in me when Steven died, and I didn't know who I was anymore. They stood by me as I fumbled to find my footing. They made me feel that who I was – and who I had been – was good and still alive. No words to express.

Part 1

Steven and Meredith

BEGINNING WITH AN ENDING

I often say, "When I met Steven, I died."

First, it was at a suicide prevention training program, where he encouraged me to lie down, imagine myself at my own memorial, and speak my last words to the people I loved. This dropped me deeper into my awareness of the poignancy of death, around which Steven and I shared a lifelong fascination. There would be many death experiences over our lifetime together that would inform our lives and work. This was the first.

But something else in me died when I met Steven. The life I had lived up to that point – my young life – completely fell away. Meeting Steven began an entirely new phase of my life. I stepped into my womanhood, and everything changed.

MEREDITH

I was brought up in the country with a lot of family, and I was a shy, introverted young girl. I had my own horse, and I was outside pretty much all the time. I like to think I was really raised by horses.

We lived in rural Minnesota, so in the winter it was skiing, and in the summer, it was riding or exploring. Being outside was where I escaped the tension of home, and it's where I loved to be.

Nature was the place where I felt connected. I have a memory of lying in a field of clover looking up at the swift clouds, and feeling that, for just a few moments, everything was connected. Everything was one. It was one of those "A-ha!" moments as a child. I think just about every child, if given the right environment, has those experiences. It wasn't any big revelation, it just was. I felt that down to my bones. I still hold the flavor of that memory.

My grandparents were from Pennsylvania, and my Grandfather came from a family of Pennsylvania Dutch Dunkards. Like the Amish, they were very simple people. They grew all their own food and made all their own clothes.

My grandfather was said to be a very humble man, from a very simple background. He was the first person in his lineage to graduate from college, and he had to fight for that. His parents did not want their kids to go to college. But he did. He became a bank president, founded a newspaper, and became an incredibly successful and prominent man in Bethlehem, Pennsylvania. According to my mother, however, he was not much good at being a father. I think I identified with his lineage of simplicity and connection to the land, although I was very young when he died.

When I was seven years old, my parents divorced. My father, Alden "Aldie" Hine, fell in love with our neighbor, Ginnie, who lived across the cornfield with her husband, Phil. After a year of painful and deeply honest conversations between the couples, my mother and Phil realized that they too had fallen in love. So my father and Ginnie and her four children lived up the hill. My mother, Phil, and the four children in our family lived down the hill. Each couple had one more child, and we grew up like one big family.

The love between my father and Ginnie was so strong. I saw the love they had for each other, and I felt the love they had for me. I also saw how their love together gave them the courage to dedicate their lives to what they loved doing. Eventually they moved to Florida to pursue the professions that they really loved – Ginnie a professor of social anthropology, and Aldie a professor of marine microbiology. They were incredibly interesting people, and they had a flow-through house where people loved being around them. Ginnie especially, being a social anthropologist, was always into interesting conversations.

I don't think I ever really said to myself, "I want that kind of relationship." But I knew, because I was a part of that family and of that love, what it looked like and what it felt like. I had it in my bones.

Before my parents divorced, we sometimes went to church, where my father loved to sing in the choir. But this was the 1950s, and after the divorce, they were kicked out of the church. So I did not get raised in a family that went to church much.

But at the age of about 10 or 11, I became very interested in religion. My mother used to drop me off at different churches every Sunday. Some of them were absolutely boring, some of them were interesting, and each of them touched my yearning to have some understanding of that world. Later my mother introduced all of us to the Unitarian Church, and some of us went to Sunday School there.

All my parents loved and trusted me, and that was important. My mom had five children, and she gave us a lot of freedom. Where we lived in the countryside was a safe place then, and I grew up very self-reliant. As I look back now, I'm sure a lot of the work I've dedicated my life to doing came from that time. I had the sense that all religion and all spirituality came out of the land. When I was outside I felt whole, and this relationship helped me through the ups and downs of childhood and adolescence.

In the mid-1960s, our family moved to Mill Valley, CA, right as the "hippie revolution" and the Vietnam protests were happening. Living in the San Francisco Bay Area was a big change from rural Minnesota. It was an exciting time that challenged many of the basic assumptions in our culture and, at 15 years old, a perfect time for me as

I was beginning to develop my values.

I went to a very good private girl's school for my final three years of high school, where I had to work hard, especially because grades didn't come easy for me. I was immersed in creative conversations with other girls who were more adept at getting high grades, while at the same time respecting each other's thoughts. It was here that I came to love to learn.

I went away to college at the University of California at Santa Barbara in the late 1960s. I quickly became frustrated with college because it was all just words, and I didn't know how to make it real. This was a time of believing, "if it's not real, it's not authentic," and "if I don't live my truth, life feels meaningless."

In 1970, the students held a violent protest against the Vietnam War and burned the Bank of America building. There was fire in the streets, army trucks, and soldiers roaming the town all night to enforce the curfew, actually shooting at students. I remember walking through the streets all night throughout the many protests, trying to understand my own relationship with protest and violence. It heightened that sense of, "I don't know where the world is going." I didn't know if we were going to survive.

During that time, I felt that the only meaningful education was experiential education, so I really wanted to create my own major. I loved studying Spinoza and Taoism, and I loved philosophy, psychology, mythology, and sociology. But if I couldn't see how one could apply it in a meaningful way, it was just a mind thing. I got involved in encounter groups, and I started leading certain groups that I got college credit for.

I said to the University, "I want to make my own major." And they said, "Well, get into the Scholars Program." I got in the Scholars Program, which was supposed to provide more opportunities for intensive study. But they still wouldn't let me design my own major.

So I left the University, moved back to the Bay Area, found a place to live in the little town of Inverness, and went to Antioch College West, a school where you can create your own education. I designed my own major and called it, "Human Responsibility: our ability to respond to ourselves, to each other, and to the earth."

STEVEN

Steven was conceived in a little stone house in the middle of the desert northeast of Los Angeles, where his father had a small gold mine. To create a better home for the family, his parents moved a little closer to Los Angeles, first to the town of Acton, and then to Burbank.

Steven's father was a gold miner, and his mother also grew up in a little gold mining town. He was raised by parents who loved the mountains and deserts. They often went fishing in the Sierra or hiking and exploring the Owens Valley, which at that time was up a dirt road from LA. Many of the important memories of his childhood come from those times in the outdoors.

I don't know much about Steven's lineage. He never really knew a lot of his ancestors. Some of them came from Germany, and he felt very connected with that ancestry. His father's line was quite intellectual. One of his ancestors was the first woman to graduate from the law school she attended.

His mother's family was Fundamentalist Christian, and that's how Steven was raised. Sin and guilt were important teachings. They were the kind of Christian that, if they opened a book that in any way threatened their faith, they closed the book.

So Steven grew up being a really good Christian boy. He got the love of his parents, especially his mother, by being a good Christian boy. He'd go out into the streets with his father and the Bible to try and convert other people. He went to a good Christian college, and he married the daughter of the headmaster. He really wanted to live the life that made him loved by his parents.

One year after he married a really decent and fine Christian woman, he fell in love with another woman who was way edgier, and that began a time of incredible rebellion. He went to the opposite extreme from being a good Christian boy to a rebel. From then on, his mother admitted to him that she wasn't sure she could love him. That was very painful for Steven, and in some ways, it made him push the edges even harder. He was always searching to break free of the guilt and shame that haunted him.

Even though Steven eventually left the Christian church, he was a deeply spiritual man. He believed that Jesus was an example to strive towards. I don't want to make this sound strange, but he wanted to get as close to being a kind of Jesus as he could. In his parents' religious faith, for anybody to even think that they could be anything like Jesus, was an abomination. "We are born sinful," they said. To even wish that you could have some of the qualities of Jesus was a sin.

Part of the tension that followed Steven throughout his life came from feeling torn between two generations. He was raised in the 1940s and 1950s by a very traditional World War II, Fundamentalist Christian family. On the other hand, he came into his own in the 1960s during a new era of hippies, free love, drugs, and the Vietnam War.

Steven graduated cum laude from Westmont College in Santa Barbara in 1960 with a double major in Literature and Psychology. He got a PhD in English Literature and Humanities from the University of Washington, and he taught at the University of Washington, the University of Wyoming, and finally at San Francisco State University.

At San Francisco State, he was one of the most loved professors for his outrageously creative classes. He became deeply involved with student and faculty groups in protesting the Vietnam War, and he was ultimately fired in 1971, along with a lot of other professors, for his involvement in the war protests.

Around that time, he divorced his second wife, and he went back out into the Mojave Desert to figure out what to do with his life. It was in shambles – divorce, leaving his children, losing his job. Off and on for a year he went out into the desert to ask, "Who am I now? What am I going to do?"

The desert was the place where he felt his truth could be found.

FRIENDSHIP

Part of the college degree I designed for myself was to work at Marin Youth Advocates, an organization dedicated to preventing child abuse and advocating for the best interests of children, and write up the experience. My plan also took me to the Marin Suicide Prevention Center in San Anselmo, where I was invited to volunteer on the phones after a pretty extensive training program.

In 1972, after a year of volunteering, they invited me to be a trainer. That's when I met Steven. He had been invited to come and offer one of the once-a-month ongoing training programs for volunteers, because they had heard he did some creative death and dying experiences both when he was a professor at San Francisco State and at Marin Open House, where he then worked with at-risk kids. As part of the training, he asked for someone to lie down and imagine they were at their own memorial.

I was really shy, but nobody raised their hand. I really wanted to do it, so I finally volunteered. He told me to imagine that people had one last chance to come and say goodbye to me, and that I had one last chance to say goodbye to them. He helped me identify the important people in my life and guided me into the feelings of what I would say to them if this was my end. This dropped me deeper into the awareness of the poignancy around death, which I would later learn was a fascination that Steven and I shared.

Steven was a trainee himself, and at the end of his training group, the staff got together to decide who to invite to volunteer on the phones. When they got to Steven, they didn't know what to do with him. He didn't follow any of the rules, but there was something about him that they all agreed was good.

They decided to put him on my overnight shift once a week so I'd watch over him, even though I was 13 years younger than he was. So for the next year, once a week, from 11 at night to 7 in the morning, together we answered phone calls from people who wanted to die.

As we listened to the calls that came in, we realized that most of these people didn't really want to die. What they really hungered for was some kind of meaningful, symbolic death that would bring healing to a life that felt so full of despair. What they really wanted was to find a way to make peace with their life up to that point so they could move on. They felt held back by their past and trapped, like in a box canyon. They thought physical death was their only way out.

During that year, Steven had begun to take groups of at-risk kids out into the desert through Marin Open House. He experimented with how to create a meaningful event for young people to mark their passage into adulthood. We talked a lot about how we should bring this not only to young people, but also to adults. We talked a lot about what it meant to die, both physically and symbolically.

One night, I arrived at the center after I'd been to a party, and I was feeling good. Just before our shift started, I received a phone call from my stepmother, Ginnie, who told me that my father was diagnosed with cancer.

I adored my father. I hadn't lived with him since I was seven, but I adored him, and I started sobbing. It was Steven who helped me through the night. He was the one who was there for me.

At the end of that year of volunteering together, both Steven and I decided we'd had enough of working at the center. We looked at each other and said, "Well, wait a minute. We still want to see each other." After a year of sharing those nights, we had developed a deep trust in one another and had become good friends. We also connected over a shared love of being outside on the land.

We were both working for federally funded programs that served youth – Steven at Marin Open House, and me at Marin Youth Advocates. Each time Steven returned from one of his wilderness programs, we'd go out for coffee. He'd just sit there and cry about these groups of kids he was taking out into the desert. He didn't know what was happening, but it was changing these kids tremendously. He would just cry.

I thought what he was doing was such an authentic and meaningful challenge. I had always felt that education should be experiential, and the things I was most interested in combining at college – sociology, religious studies, mythology, psychology – were the same elements he was applying experientially. I had gotten my degree by bringing those things together in ways that I felt were creative. Now here was Steven, bringing them together in an experiential way.

FALLING IN LOVE

I had a little blue Volkswagen Karmann Ghia convertible, and we decided to drive into Nevada for two weeks. Many people think that Nevada is just empty, but there are wonderful old ghost towns, old mines, and vast open lands scattered with signs of earlier people. We just followed our whim. We looked for arrow points, explored old mining camps, found hot springs out in the middle of nowhere, walked the mountains and flats, and threw our sleeping bags down wherever we ended up at the end of the day.

We realized that we were falling in love. Steven played the banjo, and during those two weeks, he wrote beautiful songs about falling in love.

When we came back, I knew I had to go and see my father. So I got in my little blue Ghia again and drove across the country to spend some time with Aldie and Ginnie in Florida. I drove all day, and just pulled off on some dirt road and threw my sleeping bag on the ground to sleep.

There was so much richness in that time. I was 23 years old, and it was the first trip that I was really on my own. Those three weeks were filled with the experience and self-understanding that came with being a single woman traveling alone. I rarely talked to anybody except the occasional, wonderfully unexpected encounters. And I was being called home by my dying father.

After visiting my father and Ginnie, I drove up the East Coast to see my brother at Duke University. There was a letter waiting for me there, from Steven. He was a man of such emotion and passion. In the letter, he talked about how he felt like he'd found the woman of his life, and that he didn't want to lose me.

I had been driving day after day, camping anywhere, not eating much, and being full of my father. I got this letter at a time when I was very vulnerable, and everything was so unknown. It was the sense you get when you know that someone you love is about to die. I was falling in love in a way that I'd never fallen in love before, and it was a bit frightening. All I could do was say to myself, "I have to just trust," not knowing what was going to happen, and not needing to know what was going to happen. I was losing the most important man in my life, my father, and I was falling in love for the first time. Both of them made me feel like there was no way to control any of it. I just had to ride it, and not be afraid to love and to grieve, both, as deeply as I needed to.

When I got that letter, what I read into it, partly because I was feeling so vulnerable, was "Oh my God, he's telling me that I have to make a commitment or it's going to be over." But as I drove into the night, something in me shifted. I realized, "I'm not in a place of being able to make any kind of commitment, but I do know that I love him and don't want to lose him." I knew I had to say "yes" in some big way. I had to say that this was not just a passing thing, but that the relationship was serious.

Then I thought, "Okay, what am I doing driving up the East Coast?" I turned and headed west.

A few days later, I pulled into Steven's place in Sausalito. He was just packing up to take a group of heroin addicts out into Nevada to do a three-day-and-night solo fast through Marin Open House. He simply said to me, "Come."

So I threw my backpack into his truck, and it became the first trip that I really got to see what he was doing, to really watch how this experience affected these seven young men who were on a methadone program. They went out, found solo spots, made stone piles, and every morning the nurse who went with us would go to each stone pile and leave their methadone for the day.

When they came back in on the fourth morning, it was my first chance to really get a feeling for what Steven was doing. I'd listened to his stories, but it was my first chance to see the eyes of these young men as they came back in. I didn't know what had just happened, but it was something big.

Steven and I decided to live together when we came back from that trip. I moved into his tiny apartment in the hills of Sausalito, with the roll of the ocean and the view of the beautiful San Francisco Bay.

"We don't know where it's going to lead," we said, "but we're going to turn into it, and we're going to trust it."

That was our commitment.

ALDIE'S DEATH

Several months after we moved in together, Ginnie called to say that my father had only a little bit of time left. I quickly flew back to Florida to be with my father for his last two weeks. Steven was able to come for the last several days, and so we shared one of the most important experiences of my life up to that point: my father's death.

I think death changes us, no matter how it comes. At Aldie's death, I learned to support someone's dying in a way that was very different from the culture at that time: surrounded by family at home, before hospice was available. It was a very intimate time, and a very big teaching.

The loss of my father was the first big loss of my life. Sharing that with Steven, who turned out to be my one real love, was the beginning of a lifetime of sharing death and losing people we cared about.

During that time with my family, Steven also got a sense of the relationship between my father and Ginnie. He quickly came to love Ginnie, and she loved him. She talked a lot while we were there about what she called "bonded couples," which is what she called the deep love that she and Aldie shared. I saw how strongly Steven yearned for that kind of commitment and love.

I wouldn't realize until I read some of his early journals after he died, what a huge shift in his life happened when we met and fell in love. Really, it was a marking moment for Steven. He wanted so badly to have a relationship where the foundation was solid, where he felt loved unconditionally.

Here he was, the ultimate playboy. But what he really was looking for was a family, love, and to make a significant impact on the world. And when he saw the kind of love between my father and Ginnie, he said, "I want you to marry me because you know this kind of love." After we got married he often said, "Finally, I have that solid foundation of our relationship. Now I can go and do my life's work."

TRIP TO BAJA

During that year we were falling in love, Steven and I took my little Ghia down to Baja to camp out on the beach. At that time, there was this incredible, long white-sand beach next to the little village of Mulege called The Bay of Conception. All that was on this beach were a couple of little fishing villages. We thought, "This would be a great place to bring a group." So we began to plan a trip to take a group of kids down to Baja.

When we got back home after my father's death, we continued talking about this crazy idea, and we decided to do it. As part of his work at Marin Open House, Steven went into the schools – often the continuation and alternative schools because they were more welcoming – to do programs with young people. It was one of the ways he got them interested in coming with him to fast in the desert.

So together we began to go to different schools. We mostly went to schools where there were at-risk kids, both because they were such interesting kids, and because their schools had the most freedom of education. You could bring new things into the schools that regular schools would have a lot more resistance to.

We decided that a really good way – a therapeutic way – of supporting these wonderful kids was to create a situation that we knew would turn into a crisis. We thought this would be a hands-on, experiential way of teaching them how to live with other people, work together as a community, and be responsible. It would also support their passing into adulthood by bringing in qualities that were needed in adulthood.

So we told each of them to bring only $50 dollars for three weeks. We knew that they were going to run out of money, and we consciously planned it that way. When there's a crisis, either the best or the worst qualities come out in people. They would have to work together to feed themselves.

We prepared the kids to get ready, to learn how to fend for themselves, how to be a community, how to drink responsibly, how to be respectful of another culture, and how to deal with crisis. We talked a lot about community and different roles in communities. And they learned a lot about the culture and environment of Baja and Mexico.

The Superintendent of Schools, a woman who was the head of a number of schools, got wind of what we were trying to do. She didn't like it at all. She thought it was way too risky, and she didn't want to take on the liability. "It's a crazy idea," she said, and she made moves to shut it down.

Steven called all the parents, got them together, and let them know what we were doing and why we were doing it. He told them that the Superintendent was trying to stop us.

Immediately the parents got behind it. They saw the value of what the teaching could be, as Steven was able to so artfully describe it, and for some crazy reason, they actually trusted us to do it. This was in the 1970s. I don't think we'd get that kind of support today.

One of the parents was a lawyer, and he went to the Superintendent and told her that the parents had decided they were going to let their sons and daughters go with us. And if it couldn't be done through the school, then it was okay with them that the kids were playing hooky for three weeks. And if she didn't want to give them credit for school (and receive the per diem that schools receive for each child in attendance), that was up to her.

In the end, she had to allow it, asking that the students hand in a report on their experiences when they returned.

Then we had to find a way to get them all down there. We drove around Marin County looking for a bus. We came to a great big parking lot, and there was an old rickety school bus and a man who was living in the bus. We said, "Hey, you wanna come down to Baja with us?" "Sure," he said. "I'm not doing anything else."

We had a lot of work to do to fix up the bus. It had a lot of mechanical problems. We added water tanks and put in some beds. It would have to serve as home to us and 30 kids for three weeks.

On the trip, we blew tires right and left, we ran out of food, some of the kids blew their money right away on booze, we got stopped by the policia and searched, there was mutiny, scavenging for food from the ocean and the fishing villages, and there was love. I remember looking down the seats at the kids talking with each other, eating moldy tortillas because that's all they had. It was an incredible adventure for young people learning how to be resourceful and live in community.

We didn't do a lot of directing. Instead, we allowed the teaching to come out of what was happening. Some of the kids went out and got very drunk. And we said, "Look what you're doing. Look how this is affecting the whole community." We had the teachable moment come from an actual situation they'd created themselves. It was true experiential learning.

We tried to make it a community journey, and we stayed somewhat in the background. Obviously, we made final decisions, but we didn't rule the roost. We needed them to take charge. Anyone could call a meeting at any time. There was a lot of gossip among them, and they got to see that spreading rumors created trouble in the whole community. Some began to take on real leadership roles. They began to see the best and the worst in themselves.

We also played a lot with ceremony. Kids love ceremony. There was no drinking age in Mexico at that time, but there were soldiers everywhere who could stop you for no reason. Again, this is back in the 1970s. Smoking marijuana was common. If you got caught with drugs, you went to jail.

So before crossing the border, we stopped and did a little ceremony, where everybody, including Steven, had to throw away their dope. "Everybody," he said, "if you've got dope in your pocket, we're going to go over there and dig a hole, and we're going to bury it. We're doing this together. That's our commitment to each other."

Along the way, we did other little ceremonies. We called a meeting every morning and drew a Tarot card, which would be the theme of the day. We did little things like that. Mostly we responded when chaos began to happen. Someone would call a group meeting and we'd do council. And when something good happened, we'd come together and celebrate.

The night we got to the Bay of Conception, it was dark. A lot of the kids were drunk. We'd blown two tires trying to go cross country to get to the beach. We had with us a wonderful German couple, Rolf and his girlfriend Sunshine, who had a Jeep. They'd heard about our adventure and offered to come with us. They'd gone ahead to find the beach, but in the dark, they'd gotten too close to the water and were completely stuck in the sand.

So there we were, hobbling behind with a blown tire. We finally reached the beach around 2 in the morning, and there were Rolf and Sunshine with their Jeep completely stuck. Our kids were tired and sick, but we called them all together and said, "Everybody off the bus. We've got to get the Jeep out."

Just before dawn, we had to admit that we were not going to get it out that night. Finally, everyone got their sleeping bag and found a spot on the beach. Steven and I grabbed our sleeping bags and started walking down the beach, as far away from the kids as we could get. We were so tired of them by then.

As we were walking down the beach, we looked on the eastern horizon where it was just beginning to get a little bit lighter. And there was a comet, a beautiful comet that was stretched all the way across the sky.

Here we were on this beautiful beach, with the ocean and the sunrise and the comet, and even though the trip was absolute chaos, we were doing it together. We looked at each other and Steven said, "Okay, under this comet, I commit my life to you, all the way to the end. And beyond. This is who we are together for the rest of our lives."

We had set that group up to be chaos. We knew the bus would break down many times – and it did. We knew we would need everybody to get us through – and they did. They found food, they made friends with fishermen, they dug clams, and they really got to see themselves and how they were a part of the community. Who were the ones that went and found food for the group? Who were the ones that tried to divide the group? And who were the ones who brought the community together?

A year later, when we were living in Greece, Steven wrote a full-length (still unpublished) manuscript about that time, called All the Way to Mulege. We made sure that all the kids kept journals, and at the end of the trip, we asked those who were willing to give them to us to read. Pretty much all of them did. When we read their journals, we found out a lot more about what was going on in the background. The book is full of excerpts from their journals, and our journals, that Steven wove together into a beautiful story.

The trip was very challenging. Yet the whole time, somehow it was all okay. Chaos was something that felt creative. It was not in itself a bad thing. Steven and I learned that, together, we were capable of holding chaos, allowing it to turn into opportunities for teaching and healing, and still keep people safe.

It amazes me that, in all these years, we've had so few accidents and so few real crises, because I know my life with Steven was about walking the very thin line between safety and taking risks. Putting people out on the land without food, and knowing that we had no control over what was going to happen, that's walking a thin line.

But it's being willing to walk that line, to take risks, that changes us. It grows us. It matures us. We find out who we are by taking risks.

That Baja trip was a test of what crisis would do to Steven and me. We realized that our personalities were very different, but they worked well together. It was a crazy trip, a really hard trip, we got sick of the kids a lot, but never once did it threaten to divide us. We got stronger together than we were individually. And it made us closer.

THE ODYSSEY

One of the things that Steven and I discovered about each other was that Homer's Greek epic poem, *The Odyssey,* had been important in both our lives. At various times, each of us had separately said to ourselves that we would love to be able to follow Odysseus to Ithaca, to find home. How wonderful it was when we discovered that we shared the same dream. So we decided to do it together.

The trip to Greece was about two things: partly it was to follow a shared dream. It was also about having the space to decide what we wanted to dedicate our lives to. We were young, and we had that feeling that anything was possible, especially if we did it together. We didn't have much money, but had plenty of love to share. We felt that we could do anything with this love between us. But what was it that we wanted to put our love toward?

We decided that if we were going to Greece, we didn't want to decide exactly where we were going to go. If we wanted to find "home" like Odysseus did, we'd have to go down there looking for it. And we would stay until we were done.

We flew to Belgium, and there was a young man at the airport who was selling his van. For a couple hundred dollars, we bought the van and started out. We decided to bring along Steven's son, Keenan, for part of the trip. At 11, he was the perfect age.

We had a month before Keenan flew into London. So for a month, Steven and I just wandered around Europe, camping out, letting ourselves be drawn to where we felt like we wanted to go. We had very little money, but we didn't need much. Steven wrote some beautiful banjo songs along the Mosel and the Rhine rivers. We camped out, we got cheese and bread, and we had our love. It was a good time.

After a month, we drove to London, picked up Keenan, and immediately headed for Greece. We drove down the length of what was still Yugoslavia, and at Kotor, our van broke down. Kotor was the most beautiful place in what was then the southern part of Yugoslavia. It was just a small little village, and we found a guy who worked on cars. We had to stay there for two weeks, waiting for money to be sent from my stepfather through Western Union, so we could pay to get our van back. We camped on the most beautiful beach, and the people in the village were so good to us.

Finally, the van was fixed, and we drove up and over the mountains, down into northern Greece. We made our way to Athens and began to island hop. We tried out many of the little villages, and in the end, we took the ferry to Ithaca, a little rocky island. There were only two other cars on the island besides ours, and after getting off the ferry at the small fishing village of Vathi, we took a winding dirt road up and over the island and down to the little town of Kioni on a beautiful little cove. The three of us sat in the taverna on the edge of the water, looking out at this gorgeous little bay, and we smiled at each other and said, "Home!"

We had learned just enough Greek to get by, so we asked the taverna owner, "Is there any place to rent?" He went and got an old Greek man, Nicolas, who owned the falling-down building right behind the taverna. At that time, there was no electricity in the village except for one strand – one television in the taverna, a wind-up telephone, and a generator.

Our new home was a sweet little white-washed stone two-story, with nothing in it but an old wooden table and a little bed. There was no running water, no plumbing, and no heat. There was a tiny balcony outside the upstairs bedroom that looked out on the sea, and there was a well outside the front door that the taverna used for their water. Once a week, with one gallon of water each, we went outside to wash our hair and bodies.

Keenan loved it there. The villagers couldn't believe what a big, strong 11-year-old he was, and they got all excited when he went diving and brought up an octopus. They showed him how to pound the octopus to cook it, and he became part of the village. We didn't know the culture, and we made a lot of mistakes. But the people were good to us. We all missed Keenan when he returned to Athens and then home to school.

During that time, Steven worked on his manuscript for *All the Way to Mulege*. Then there were a couple of days when I wasn't feeling well. Steven went down to the taverna to look for Dionysios, a fisherman who spoke English and had taken us under his wing.

"I don't know what's wrong," Steven said. "She's sick!"

"We're going to get in your car and drive to Vathi," Dionysios said. "We're going to see the Mam`i."

We drove to the clinic with him, where the "baby doctor" gave me a pregnancy test. It came out positive.

Dionysios was so excited. From that point on, we found little piles of fresh fish he had caught that morning, or fruit at the back door. It was so sweet.

That same day we found out I was pregnant, two young Greek brothers who had also become friends took us out night fishing in their little boat. It was really calm and there was a huge full moon hanging over the bay. It was one of those nights that was just magic.

We asked them, "How do you say 'moon' in Greek?" And they told us, "i Selene." We said, "Okay, if we have a girl, we're going to call her Selene."

"No, no, no!" they said. "You'll have a boy! Your first one will be a boy." It seemed from then on, that was the theme. All the Greek women in their black mourning clothes would come up and pat my belly, and we'd talk about how the baby was making me sick. And they'd say, "Oh, good! That's good! It'll be a boy, then!"

Part 2

Rites of Passage

FOLLOWING A DREAM

In Greece, we decided that we wanted to dedicate our lives to bringing meaningful wilderness rites of passage experiences to people – especially young people. As an English professor, Steven had studied many myths, poems, and fairy tales. These expressed again and again the universal human story of initiation, and the importance of this ceremony in maintaining the health and balance of each individual and their communities.

In our culture, we saw how the lack of community-sanctioned rites-of-passage ceremonies handicapped our young people when it came time to find their place as adults in our society. Steven's experimentation with youth groups through Marin Open House was an early exploration into bringing rites of passage ceremonies back into the fabric of our culture.

So when we came back to Northern California in 1977, very pregnant, with no money and no jobs, we had this dream. We moved into our friend and midwife's little house on Indian Valley Road in Novato, and we got married on Mt. Tamalpais. Three months later, our baby girl, Selene, was born in front of a warm fire while Steven serenaded us with banjo music.

That same year, we officially launched the nonprofit Rites of Passage, Inc. While we were in Greece, Steven had written to Edward Beggs, the man who had hired him to be a part of what he called "Rites of Passage," the youth component of Marin Open House. Since Marin Open House was dissolving, Edward generously agreed to let us have the name.

During the next few years, we worked really, really hard going into classrooms to educate youth and teachers about rites of passage and the indigenous perspective. We both had connections with youth agencies and schools because of our earlier work, and we found the teachers who were most interested in what we were doing.

We mostly focused on alternative schools, continuation schools, social youth organizations, drug agencies that were working with youth, and programs that served at-risk kids. The mainstream schools were much more resistant, and liability was higher on their list of importance.

We were pretty "far-out" people. We were different from their usual teachers. At first, I was pregnant, and then I was caring for little Selene. We put her on the desk in the room while we talked to the kids. Or we handed her to one of them to watch. Steven was so charismatic, and it was exciting for them.

The schools didn't want to take on the liability associated with what we were doing in the field, so we took on the liability under Rites of Passage. At the end of a meeting at the school we said, "Okay, if you really want to do this, we're going to meet at our house" on a certain night. "You have to get yourself there," which wasn't always easy for them. They had to really want to come. It was mixed, girls and boys, and so a lot of the girls came to the meetings in high heels and make-up – it was a social thing.

We met with them once a week for one or two months to prepare them for the three-day solo fast in the desert. We talked a lot about how this challenge would be a chance to test themselves, and how it would make them a man or a woman. We asked, "Can you live without food for three days? Can you live without your mother and father? Can you take care of yourself when you get cold and hungry?" Of course, everybody wanted their friends to see that they could do it. They were at that age where they wanted the test. They loved the challenge.

After going out with us on their vision fast, the kids returned to school, their eyes bright. And then others wanted to do it, too. Interest grew, as it still does today, by word of mouth. We charged very little money and encouraged them to convince people in their lives to help support them. Some got temporary jobs to pay their own way.

It was a time of hard effort, a lot of love between us, and a lot of newness. We had no idea if this was going to work, but we were committed to it. From the very beginning, we were dirt poor. We did everything we possibly could to keep going. I cleaned houses, and Steven sometimes worked as a "Kelly Girl," a temporary typing secretary.

We wrote to people who liked what we were doing, who were close friends, and we asked for little bits of donations. We began to do fundraisers, just enough to keep going. For two years, we got funding from the Buck Family Fund of Marin County, which gave us a small salary. Steven learned the art of proposal writing, and he hated it.

Two of our allies at that time were Howard and Sue Lamb, two wonderful people who were consultants funded by the Buck Family Fund to bring together people from all the youth agencies in Marin County. Steven went to the meetings and represented Rites of Passage. The Lambs saw that he was an out-of-the-box person, and they fell in love with him and our work. Soon they became involved in Rites of Passage, went out on trips with us, and served on our board of directors for many years. They helped us keep the work growing, pushed us to charge enough money to sustain ourselves, and became dear friends.

The probation officers began to ask, "What are you doing with these kids? We've never seen such change." And the parents were amazed, saying, "Something has changed in them!"

We also saw big changes in these kids, just by putting them out and letting them live alone for three days without food. So we began to ask ourselves, "Well, what is it that we are doing? What is happening? And how do we support this in even better ways?"

That's when we began to look at the pan-cultural elements of an initiation, or rite of passage. And we set out to create the bones of the ceremony.

BONES OF THE CEREMONY

We began to explore more deeply, "What is it that indigenous people did and still do?" We carried that question for years, and it was bottomless: "How do you hold ceremonial space? How do you put people out on the land and receive them back?" We began to educate ourselves and experiment with different ways. It always felt bottomless.

As we researched indigenous people from around the world, we saw that solo time was a common ingredient in this kind of ceremony: young people being taken away from their mothers, fathers, and community to find what was important to them.

Another common and important element of the ceremony was the aspect of feeling pushed to the edge: that place of risk, that place of feeling as if they might die.

For modern people, going without food and being alone in nature created the edge that was so scary for them, that they felt as if they might die. That element seemed really important in awakening the initiation ceremony.

We began with those very simple bones: solo time, no food, no company, no artificial shelter. We tried to keep it as simple as possible. That seemed to be the best way to learn what the ceremony itself brought out in people.

So when young people came off their solo, they felt as if they'd really done something big. We saw how important it was to them to prove to themselves, as well as their peers and parents, that they were capable of doing this. They were proving that they could do something so scary and survive it all alone.

We began playing with ceremony. We loaded them up on a bus and drove through the night to Death Valley, or to the Inyos, or the White Mountains. When we arrived after driving all night and walking several miles into base camp, the kids were exhausted. We were in this foreign place, and we knew that we needed to do some kind of ceremony to help everyone "arrive." So before anything else, we stopped and made a circle, and everyone poured out some water and gave thanks to the place.

We tried other simple things too, like making a circle for them to step through when they went out on solo time, and having them step back in when they returned. We played with how ceremony supported what we were doing with the kids.

In those early days, we sat with each person on the long bus ride home and asked, "What happened out there? How did it go?" We just let them talk. We knew it was good for them to talk about it, but there was learning in it for us, too. We needed to know what worked and what didn't work.

As we listened to the stories of people who came off solo, we began to see which components were the most important. We also saw that some of the things we tried to include only got in the way and stifled creativity. We began to understand that the power of the ceremony was in its simplicity. It was what happened between the faster and the ceremony when they were alone in the desert.

THE POWER OF INTENTION

Slowly, we began to build a reputation. Before long, judges were saying to kids who had gotten in trouble, "Either you go to Juvenile Hall, or you go and do that program in the desert."

At first we thought, "God, that's good!" But then we began to see what was happening. Of course they chose to come with us instead of going to Juvenile Hall. Who wouldn't?

So they came out with us, they did their three days and nights alone, and they had a good time. They did it really well, they enjoyed it, and they came back feeling fine. Then they went back to their old life.

I remember one story that was the turning point for us. There was a young man who broke into houses and stole things. He came and did three days and nights, no problem. He'd never camped before, and he loved it. Then he went back home, and articles began to appear in newspapers about night burglaries. After several months, the police finally found this young man camping up in the hills. He had put up a tent and created a little home hidden in the woods. At night, he snuck down and broke into houses. After the vision fast, he wasn't afraid of the dark anymore.

We realized that, although the vision fast is always good for them, you can't just say, "This will be good for you, so you need to do it." It has to come from the young people themselves. They needed to feel called to do this. They needed to have a pretty good reason to do it if they were going to get through it, because it wasn't easy. Three days and nights alone without food is hard. If they didn't have a good reason to do it, they came back into base camp early.

Some of the kids told us they just wanted to try it out. They said it sounded like fun, their friends were doing it, and they wanted to do it, too. We began to see that these kids usually didn't make it through the whole solo time. That was a really important understanding for us. That was the beginning of the "commitment statement" and "creating intent" that was necessary for the fast to be truly meaningful.

Steven and I focused on their intention because we needed to hear, "I want to do this. This is important to me." We needed to hear that they were ready to die to childhood and step into adulthood.

We also realized from studying initiation fasts around the world, that these kinds of ceremonies are confirmatory. They are a way for the young person, as well as community, to confirm and acknowledge that this person is no longer a child. It's about dying to childhood. There's no going back. They're being born back into a whole new life, world, name, role, and responsibility. At its core, the ceremony confirms the dying of the child and the birth of the adult.

We began to see how important it was to bring that strong message to the youth. We said, "When you come back, you're no longer a child. When you come back and make mistakes, you're making them as an adult." We wanted to emphasize that, and empower them in setting the intent to step fully into their adulthood. The more we did that, and the more we focused on the old ways, the more we began to understand the power of intention.

Later, as our work expanded to include vision fasts for adults, we saw that there are many other natural transitions in a human life that this ceremony confirms – dying to one phase of life and stepping into a new phase. All our losses, beginning with the biggest, my father's death, completely informed our understanding of the work we were doing. As the years went by, we learned more and more about how to guide people through that symbolic death and rebirth.

From the beginning, we realized that what we were trying to return to the culture was a ceremony, a ritual. We kept asking ourselves, "How do we do this in a way that stays true to the essence of this ritual? How do we hold it as an important spiritual marking rather than a purely psychological one?"

THE SEVERANCE PHASE

One of the books that informed us deeply was *Rites of Passage,* published in 1909, by Arnold van Gennep, a Dutch-German-French anthropologist. He was one the first to study indigenous people around the world, and to notice the rituals attached to various life transitions. He found that there were three uniform phases in most of these rituals, and that they fell into a certain order. He called them "the rites of passage."

The three main phases are severance (dying to what was), threshold (stepping into the in-between place and undertaking a challenge), and incorporation (taking on a new life and integrating back into the community).

The more we learned about rites of passage, the more we saw very little acknowledgement and understanding of it in our culture. We realized that the work we were doing out in the desert, the three-day solo fast, was the threshold phase – the in-between place of the ordeal. We felt we were doing pretty well with that. But what we didn't have in place yet, and what we were constantly trying to bring in, were the severance and incorporation phases. We saw how important it was that we guided people through those two phases as well.

In indigenous cultures, the severance phase begins at a very young age as the elders prepare children for skills they'll need as adults. The children are being readied for the time when elders will take them away from their mother, father, and the community and put them into the challenges of the threshold stage. The severance gives them the skills and understanding to face the challenges of the ordeal, of leaving their childhood behind and stepping into adulthood.

So we asked ourselves, "How do we begin to simulate the severance phase? How do we prepare our young people for the ceremony of letting go of their old identity?" Again, our way was through experimentation.

We saw that, for young people, it was really difficult to put words to how they felt. They were just learning how to do that. So in the middle of our living room, we had a big pile of beautiful rocks. They were all different colors, different shapes, and various textures. As the kids came in, we said, "Okay, find a stone that represents who you are," or "how you see yourself as an adult." At another meeting we said, "Find a stone that represents your fear." Or, "find a stone that represents your relationship with your parents." We sat on the floor in a circle, and one by one they went around and described their stone.

There are a thousand different ways to describe a stone. The way they described their stones was a mirror of how they felt, how they saw themselves. Right there, from the beginning, we brought in that sense of how nature mirrors us, and how we mirror nature. They heard themselves saying some pretty amazing things. We didn't comment at all on what they said. We just said an affirmatory, "Ho!"

During those meetings, we talked about what it meant to let go of childhood. We asked, "What does that mean to you, to let it go? How does that change your relationship with your parents?" We never said, "Okay, let us tell you what it means to be an adult." We asked them, "What does it mean *to you* to be an adult? Each of you has a different way."

That also opened up a safe space to talk about things we knew they were thinking about at their age — love, sex, drugs. In doing that, we saw that we could help prepare them with tools for their adulthood: listening to other opinions, forming their own values, and taking responsibility for their feelings and their dreams.

There was no right or wrong. Rather than being therapeutic or treatment oriented, it was about being witnessed. It was about being heard and respected without being judged. It was a way for them to be with each other and talk about meaningful things that they could never say to each other before. We saw that they hungered for this, but they hadn't known how to do it. By watching us, they began to find tools they could use to listen to each other. It was a very strong experience for them, and they loved it.

As we were listening, we were also getting a sense of whether or not these kids would be safe when they were alone. We began to see that our role was to evoke these conversations so that they could explore their values and dreams. We also wanted to make sure they were going to be physically, psychologically, and spiritually safe. At least as safe as we possibly could make it.

If we felt that we couldn't trust one of them, or we felt like they were going to be a liability, we took them aside. They had to know that, if they covered their fear in boastfulness about how unafraid they were, we worried about them and what they might do when they were alone and afraid. If they could honestly speak about their fear, this automatically made them safer. They had to hear that, and they had to convince us that they were going to be safe.

Of course, youth groups are always a liability. We could never know what a young person might do. I remember being out with one group, when all of a sudden, we heard this loud crashing sound. Down the canyon comes one of the kids limping.

"What happened?" we asked. "Oh, a scorpion jumped out at me, and made me fall off a cliff." We saw this too often: kids creating some kind of emergency so they could come back in because it was just too scary or too boring being out there alone. By creating a legitimate reason to come in, they could save face.

Seeing this happen again and again taught us how to recognize the signs before they went out. One of the questions we began to ask them was, "What would bring you in? What might happen that's going to bring you in early?" And if they couldn't answer us with something real, we said, "There are good reasons to be afraid and good reasons to come in early. There is no failure in that. We need to hear that you won't macho it out when you need to come in, or create trouble as an excuse to come in."

We talked about being responsible, not only for themselves, but for their families and people. We explained how, if they got hurt out there, it would affect the whole group. The screening process around fear and responsibility was the beginning of honing their intent. We realized that one of the ways of keeping them safe was to be sure they had a real strong sense of why they were doing it, as well as a strong commitment to taking care of themselves for the good of the whole.

MIRRORING AND DEEP LISTENING

I think I was born with a certain kind of personality, and it was nurtured by having parents who really loved me – actually, four parents who really loved me, after the divorce. Even though I was very introverted and shy (still am), I seem to have been born without a lot of judgment. I've always been intensely curious and have a natural caring for other people.

Back when I was working at the suicide prevention hotline, especially before Steven became my partner, I was terrified of going in and picking up those phones. It was the only time I had nightmares about being dead. I think I've always thrived on the tension of fear, and that experience grew me.

I learned a lot by being in fear of that phone and picking it up anyway. For a full year, Steven and I shared what the work of being on those phones really meant. It was all about listening. We learned how to listen deeply, and how to listen without judgment. We couldn't fix these people. We could offer resources (for Steven that often meant playing his banjo to them for hours), and if there was an emergency, we called the police. But mostly it was listening. It was helping them get through the night by being someone who cared, and by being someone who listened to them without judgment.

That's what we carried into this rites of passage work. It was the same thing.

As an English and Humanities professor, Steven was a master at creatively critiquing stories and poetry. The combination of his ability to critique a story, and my inborn ability to listen to people without judgment, was the foundation of what we developed in the mirroring piece of listening to the initiate's story. It was the bringing together of our two gifts.

We called it "mirroring for empowerment," because, with our research and a growing understanding of how the indigenous people received initiates off the mountain, we saw that they were not looking for "what was wrong." Rather, they were listening for what appeared outside in nature, and what appeared internally in the initiate, and how these two aspects informed the wisdom of the story.

We could see that there was this dance happening between the land and the individual, as well as the greater "mystery." We began to see the relationship between the land itself and how it is constantly evoking thoughts and feelings and understandings in us.

We later learned that, around the world, there are other similar forms, such as in the Hawaiian culture, and among the Quakers, as well as Native American cultures. It was a way of listening that was not about "fixing" and wasn't problem-oriented. Rather, it was about deep listening. It goes way back. It is the old way.

As with everything else, we experimented with deep listening and mirroring. For a while we said, "Okay, you have as much time as you want to tell your story." People would go on and on, and you could feel the energy die. Pretty soon we realized that they needed a framework, like a window of time, to help them come to the essence of the story.

We also played with different ways of responding to a story. In the beginning, we didn't respond at all — we just acknowledged and empowered the story. Then for a while, we mirrored the story back and left them with one question meant to show the beginning of a movement that would continue into their life.

Then we tried to open up the story even more by asking questions to deepen the story. Nature always contains wisdom. So we might say, "What was it like when that bird came? It sounds like it was really important, that moment. What was the bird saying to you?"

Steven and I learned from each other as we heard one another practice mirroring. The process continued to grow. We began to ask ourselves, "How do we step into their stories without getting caught up in our own stories or our own value systems? How can we look around inside the story and give it back to them?"

We learned that it wasn't about fixing anyone, or solving their problems, or interpreting their story for them. The healing came from deeply listening to somebody and caring. Listening to their stories, it was so easy to just love them. I don't think you can truly mirror a story unless you do.

Indigenous people say that every physical manifestation is a piece of eternal wisdom. And so when we brush up against any manifestation around us, there is wisdom that we can touch. We asked ourselves, "How do we send them out so that they can open to sacred time and sacred space, and be receptive to the teaching of the land?"

We knew that this work was not primarily intellectual or psychological. It was clearly spiritual. It was way bigger than us. Our early teachers, the Native Americans, were very generous in sharing their way of perceiving the world. It's not about us. It's about our connection with mystery. The ceremony pointed toward the initiation of each individual into this world of spirit, feeling our connection with "the bigger."

From very early on, Steven and I realized that the ceremony had its own life. We became more and more aware that we were apprenticing ourselves to a ceremony that was constantly teaching us. So it was essential that we went out every year to do our own solo fast.

Of course, going out on our fast every year was a humbling experience. It was, and still is, a good way of recognizing and reinforcing that we are just human. We had all our human bumps and light and dreams and shadow, and it really helped keep us humble. It's pretty hard to be super-arrogant when you go out and fast every year. It also kept reminding us how it really is to go out in this way, so that it became difficult to glorify it when we spoke about it with other people or listened to their stories.

Steven and I had to stay vigilant about being in the mystery. We didn't know what Spirit wanted for this person. We might in our minds say, "Oh, I think they really need this or that." And then when they came off their solo, and we heard what actually happened, we realized that we could never have thought of a more perfect thing to happen!

The more we sent people out, and the more stories we listened to, the more we learned. And the more we got out of the way, the more we recognized that the ceremony had its own life. The guide was not the great teacher or where the wisdom was. The guide was the one to keep people safe, the one to create the simple structure to drop the initiates into, and to be there when they returned. The true wisdom was in the land.

HUMAN AND NATURE

Some of the kids we took out to the desert had never even been camping before. The archetypal acts of sleeping on the ground, building a fire, feeling the rain without shelter – these things are in our DNA. And enacting them changes us forever. So one of the things we saw changing these kids was, quite literally, sleeping on the ground. We saw the healing that takes place when we put human and nature together: waking in the night to see those trillion stars, feeling the wind, the cold, and the elements. We saw how it began to slow them down and make them more reflective, and how it also evoked feelings and aspects of their humanness that could be touched in no other way.

Living in a healthy community where each person felt seen and heard, where they felt of significance, also changed them. They were sharing something big and scary with a community of people going through the same challenges.

And the ceremony itself had its own life and teaching. The influence of being held by that ceremony obviously changed them, as well. These were the elements that comprised a life-transformative experience.

We also saw it so simply and strongly in our daughter, Selene, who was in many ways the innocent one. As an infant, she rode on our backs the 2 miles or so as we walked into base camp. She had a little doll-sized down sleeping bag that she snuggled into in a nest above our heads. One middle-of-the-night I woke up, as mothers do when their child wakes up. I looked over and her head suddenly peeked out of the little sleeping bag. She raised herself up on her knees, reached her arms up high to the sky, looking at the billions of brilliant stars.

The sight of that was so touching, I'll never forget it. There was rarely a time she woke up without crying, and this was one of them. Watching her reach up to the dark sky, and then slowly curl back down in her sleeping bag and go back to sleep, I thought, "This is what's happening to all of us."

Selene came out to base camp most of the time, from the age of a few weeks. The kids just loved it. Because we needed help with her, we told them, "She's part of the family, and you've got to help us. We've got to be in this together." Selene often wandered over to the kids and sat in their laps, or they just started playing with her spontaneously. She became a really important part of the ceremony.

We came to understand the importance of having multiple generations together. Selene added the dimension of the youngest generation. She was just a little kid, and the teenagers felt like the older brothers and sisters who were about to step into adulthood. They practiced being responsible for the young one, and it was beautiful to see. Selene loved it as well, of course.

As she got older, she became too heavy to carry on our backs. So the group went ahead with Steven, and Selene and I came behind at a much slower pace. One of the ways I tried to make it fun and keep her entertained was by asking, "Selene! What does the cactus say?" I couldn't believe the words that came out of her mouth. There was such maturity and wisdom in her answers. For her, it was easy. It was real. She'd look up at me as if to say, "Isn't it obvious? Of course the cactus talks."

This was during a time when we were learning to "deeply listen" to the land. How do we talk to trees? To birds? One of the common elements in the ceremony is the recognition that we are always in communication with the land. We went out to practice, and we learned how to develop our ability to be in communication with the world around us. We began to re-develop that part of our nature that we were born with. And then, after a while, we didn't have to practice anymore. It became a part of walking. We just walked and felt the resonance with all living things.

Selene still had that connection, whereas we were brought up hearing, "Oh, that's just your imagination." We had to work to get it back. Selene made me remember that we are born with this ability. And the young people got it right away.

Another teaching that comes out of any indigenous culture is that the sacred and profane are one. During a ceremony, there might be a sleeping grandpa in the corner and children running around and laughing. They were all a part of it. If we separated "sacred" from "profane," we'd lose the wholeness.

Selene represented that. She wandered as she wanted. She stepped into the threshold circle while we were smudging people. She was the one who often set up the circle's center – sometimes by drawing a picture and putting it in the middle – and it was all allowed. The ordinary and profane aspects of life did not ruin the quality of the sacred.

In the early 1970s, when many "New Age ceremonies" were cropping up, there was a lot of exclusiveness. I felt in some of the new age ceremonies that, if I moved the wrong way, or said the wrong thing, I would just ruin it.

This is so not how indigenous people understood it. For them, you bring everything in. We bring our humanness, and spirit does the rest. The New Age attempt at bringing the sacred back in sometimes made it more evident how we continue to live the split between sacred and profane.

FAMILY LIFE

When Selene was still a baby, we began to look for a larger home to accommodate our family and give us more room for our work.

Steven's younger son, Christian, was about five years old when we became a couple. Sometimes he was with us for summers or on weekends, and sometimes he lived with us a year at a time. Steven's older son, Keenan, also lived with us for significant periods of time, including his last years of high school. They both had good moms, and they enjoyed living between their two families.

Within a couple of months, we were blessed to find a wonderful house – one of the first houses ever built in Novato, used as a vacation home by the Melfonti family. It was still owned by Mrs. Melfonti, an elder woman who was a wonderfully creative artist. The house had beautiful ornamental gardens, an orchard, a good sized parking area, and was mostly hidden from the road. It was perfect for raising our kids, and it had an office and large living room for our meetings.

Mrs. Melfonti liked us and asked for very little rent, but we still couldn't afford it. My stepmother, Ginnie, began to give us several hundred dollars a month to help out. And a few years after my father died, she began to live with us half the year. It was such a busy time in our lives, with the phone always ringing and people in and out of the house (despite a sign on our door asking them to respect our family time in the evening). Ginnie took some of the load onto her own shoulders. We had some wonderful volunteers, but Ginnie's help was outstanding.

We were working from morning into the night, every day. One day I was in the grocery store, getting the most inexpensive, basic foods, because that was all we could afford. I remember looking at other women who were piling specialty cheeses and exotic things into their carts. It wasn't that I was angry at them. It was more a feeling of how unfair it was. We worked our butts off, and all I could give my kids were hot dogs and generic cheese.

And yet, we wouldn't have traded this life for anything. We had our love, we had creative, meaningful work, and we had our family whom we deeply loved. We were happy!

And our kids – bless them – loved us, too. Selene was too young to know that she didn't get a lot of things that other kids her age might have gotten. She was a pretty happy kid. But all of them would probably tell you we didn't stop working often enough to play.

The life we were living was much the same as having a relationship with death: knowing that we're not in control, that anything can happen any moment. Having those deep experiences around death somehow made it possible for Steven and me to take risks.

There was also something in both of us that liked being rebels. We didn't want to fit the mold. Some of that came from living through the 1960s and early 1970s. We were lucky that we were able to take some of the changing values of that time and find ways to implement and live them. I'll admit, we did have a bit of arrogance around it: "We can do this without any money at all. It's not about the money. Money is not important!"

I'm sure our children have a lot to say about that! And yet, all that made it possible for us to live this life and do this work. When we went out to do our own vision fast each year, we always asked if we should continue this work. Year after year, the answer was "yes." We were putting our values where we felt it really mattered. Because in the end, what really mattered were the people.

GINNIE'S INFLUENCE

My stepmother, Ginnie, loved what we were doing. She had always been interested, curious, and understanding of our work. As a cultural anthropologist, she had studied different cultures and their rituals. She knew that rites of passage were a key part of every indigenous culture, and that nature was an integral part of every ceremony.

As we built the foundation for Rites of Passage, Ginnie was right there with her vast cross-cultural knowledge, pointing us to the anthropological studies that supported the work we were doing. She and Steven both had that sharp intellect, and they loved arguing together – they could do it for hours. They didn't agree on everything, which was part of what was so wonderful, because it became a rich, creative conversation.

Ginnie went to a lot of our meetings and became deeply involved in our work. At the same time, she continued to create her own. She had finished her book on my father's death, *Last Letter to the Pebble People,* with an introduction by Elisabeth Kübler-Ross, and it was well received. She also became very involved in her own teaching on death and dying, and what she called "bonded couples." Even as she had been a very popular Cultural Anthropology professor at the University of Florida, I always felt her best teachings were in those last years.

Ginnie also joined us on a second trip down to Baja, where we took multiple generations together to explore community. There was little baby Selene, young Christian, some teenagers, a few people in their eighties, a gay couple, and Ginnie. She went out on fast with us quite often, and she always kept journals. We had long conversations about her story and the turmoil of emotion upon return. There was a lot of information for us as we listened to what she found when she dipped into the ceremony.

She was a very good writer. She wrote several books that are still used today (see appendix). She wrote a number of very influential articles for prominent magazines about why ritual was important, speaking about it from a cultural anthropologist's perspective. And with Steven's help, she wrote the first version of our adult and youth handbooks.

We stayed up late into the night talking about death, ritual, modern challenges, and how to deepen this work we were doing.

We talked a lot about how, in today's world, what was needed to support modern people was not to give their power away to a priest, or a guru, or a shaman, but to learn how to make meaning for themselves. We encouraged people to make their ceremonies meaningful to their own faith and value system. Ginnie wrote a manuscript on self-generated rituals so that people could, from the bare bones of pan-cultural ceremonies, get a better idea of how to create meaningful ceremony for themselves at any time in their lives.

Ginnie was key in helping us understand that all of our ancestors lived close to the land. Throughout the world, every indigenous culture created rites of passage ceremonies to support the natural life transitions in their lives. Different cultures had different "clothes" on their ceremonies specific to their communities, but they essentially served the same function in maintaining balance and health in their people and in the community.

We were certainly influenced by some Native American teachers. We could talk to them, and some were close to their lineage, whereas most indigenous people in other parts of the world were either too far away for us to go and see, or they'd lost their ceremony. The Native Americans still embodied it.

But we knew that it was important to not be focused on one particular religion or spiritual tradition. We wanted Christians and Buddhists, Atheists and Jews – all people – to bring their own meaningful symbols into the ceremony. We wanted them to bring the ceremony to life with their own meaning and cultural orientation, rather than give them symbols and actions from the Native American cosmology.

In preparing a group, we offered what seemed to be common pan-cultural elements of the ceremony for them to use (or not use) as was meaningful to their intent (such as fasting, all-night vigils, talking to the land). And we began to play with overlaying certain metaphors and symbols onto the bare bones. We did a lot of experimentation with ceremonies, and each time, we learned a little bit more. We were always asking ourselves, "How can we do it better? How could we have supported this more?"

We had a couple of Catholic nuns come through, and people of different Christian denominations, and we asked, "What are the symbols and components of your faith that you could use to make this stronger for your people?" Some of these elements included the sacrament of baptism, bringing in prayers from the Bible, and using the ceremony to mark their commitment/marriage to Jesus. It was through Ginnie's influence that we really learned how to empower others to make their ceremonies meaningful and real for themselves. It worked beautifully.

THE INCORPORATION PHASE

One of the biggest questions we continued to ask ourselves was, "How do we bring the third phase of the rites of passage – incorporation – into our modern culture?"

I remember one young man who came out of one of the continuation schools. He'd been in a lot of trouble and had been in Juvenile Hall. He did the vision fast with us, and we saw that he was a natural leader. He was really a wonderful person.

And yet, he went back to his gang and an environment that was full of drinking, drugs, and acting out. Again, we realized how important it was to find ways to reinforce their experience. So we invited him to come and assist us on another trip. We ended up doing that quite often with others, as well.

We also began to create trips that weren't vision fast trips, but focused on leadership training. This got people back out into the desert to reinforce the positive changes that were happening in their lives. This young man assisted us a number of times, and he saved my butt at one point. I was trying to find a canyon with an adult group while Steven was parking the bus way down at the bottom of the canyon. It would take him more than half the day to join us. I'm not good at directions, and we couldn't see the canyon from the horizon. This young man was the one who found it. Thank God for him!

He told us a story one night about how one of his friends had died in a car crash. He'd gathered his friends together and taken them out to a pier on the water. One by one he had them take a beer bottle, drink to their friend who had died, send a prayer and a goodbye to him, and throw the bottle out into the water. A ritual! What a beautiful way for his people, for his friends, to be able to say goodbye. People might say, "But they're drinking. And they're polluting the ocean." But really, it was genius. He found the symbol that was meaningful to his friends – and to the friend that had died.

One of the early ways we supported the incorporation phase was that, every time someone went out on vision fast with us, Steven chipped them an arrow point to wear on a chain around their neck.

And because we were working with our whole county, they might walk down the street and see somebody else with an arrowhead around their neck. Immediately they were brothers or sisters. This feeling of community was something they were hungry for. That's why our house was always full of kids.

We also began to mix "at-risk" kids with so-called "normal" kids. We found the leaders, the president of the senior class and the football hero, and we blended these high school leaders with the "juvenile delinquents" and sent them out together. They heard each other's stories and recognized some very similar feelings. It might turn out that some of the "achievers" were, in the end, sort of parasites in the community. And some of the ones who were supposedly the "bad kids" were the ones who turned out to be the leaders in the group. We created one community by blending them together, and then encouraged them to stay in contact when they got back home.

The question was always, "How do we bring community together to support the incorporation phase?" We saw that the vision fast experience did not always make life easier for them. Sometimes they came back to an environment that was not healthy for them, and often one that felt uncaring. This made it even more painful for the at-risk kids who sometimes came back to a family that didn't seem interested. They often got into even bigger trouble than before.

We talked about it with a probation officer who said, "This is actually good. These kids, they've been getting into little bits of trouble, and the parents could just send them to the probation officer. But they're coming back and they're doing something a little bit bigger so the parents have to stop and say, 'Something's not right.' And they'd have to realize that it's not just the son or daughter. It's a whole family system in trouble. By getting in more trouble, they were finally getting the help they need."

"I LET YOU GO"

We realized that one of the most important things we needed to do was prepare the kids to go back home where they might not have anybody who understood. It was so challenging to come back and not have a community to welcome you, to celebrate with you, and to say, "I see your gifts. Let me support those gifts for you and find ways to help you live those gifts." They often didn't have that once the group dispersed.

We suggested that they keep their story as a secret story. We said, "It's your power, your knowing. And if you start telling it to everybody, it can lose its power because there are people who will put it down." We warned them to be very, very careful about who they told. If they knew others who had been out with us, those were good people to find. But mostly we warned them that few people would understand or care. We encouraged them to hold their story as a thing of power. Nothing could change the significance and the importance of what they'd just done.

Some of the youth came home to very little in the refrigerator. Some came home to parents who said, "Oh, good for you, you've lost some weight!" or "Well, now you've had your vacation, go and clean the garage." Or, "If you think you're no longer a child, it's time for you to do more work around here." This was devastating for a young person who was feeling so high and full. Hearing these stories, we knew we had to begin involving the parents more.

It was clear that this rite of passage for young people was also a major rite of passage for the parents. It was a ceremonial letting go of their son or daughter into the world. This really marked a change in their family life. Sometimes they went from being a parent with kids at home to being alone with no kids at home. It was a big transition. And we knew if we could somehow help the parents be more understanding and supportive of what was happening, they could encourage their children, see them for their gifts, let them go in significant ways, and help them return to an adult life.

With Ginnie's help, we created the Parent Program. Before taking a group out, we held two meetings with the parents to explore rites of passage and talk about what they were going through as parents.

We knew that this would help them empathize with their kids. If the parents could, in a more conscious way, mark the letting go of their children, this too would support the young people. It would be pretty empowering if they were able to say, "I see you as an adult, and I let you go to your own dreams. Even though it's hard, I let you go."

We didn't want to create parent meetings that were therapeutically oriented. Again, we used the pile of stones in the middle of the living room, and when the parents arrived, we had them each choose a stone that represented their relationship with their son or daughter. Some of the parents came in suits and ties, some of them were obviously from very poor families. They were all different.

I remember one father, obviously arriving from a high- powered job, who was very uncomfortable. But he showed up! He picked a stone and described it as a dark stone that was solid and rough, that you couldn't see into. That was the symbol of his relationship with his daughter. He said so much in two minutes with that rock in his hand. I don't think he could have said that much about how he felt about his relationship with his daughter if we'd spent five hours talking. We went around the circle and each parent, with this awesome intuition, spoke to his or her relationship with their child. There was no judgment, there was no response. It was simply witnessed.

Then we asked, "Do you remember if you had a rite of passage when you were at the same age? What was your rite of passage? What did it look like?" And if they couldn't think of one, we asked, how did that feel for them? Some talked, some didn't, and it was all fine. But they all began to drop into remembering that time in their lives, and resonating with this time in the life of their child.

The parents met together again in Novato on the night that their children were enacting the all-night vigil on their third night of solo out in the desert. Usually it was Ginnie who held this meeting, because we were out with the group. The parents met that night to send good thoughts to their kids and talk about their concerns for when their son or daughter returned. We encouraged them to write down a prayer or hope that they had for their son or daughter, and let them decide for themselves whether or not to give it to them when they returned.

The last meeting was the night of the group's reunion a week after returning. First we met with the youth. We went around the circle, and they talked about how it had been since their return. Then we invited the parents to come in for a slideshow of the trip, and to share a big feast the group had put together.

In the beginning we kept it informal – the parents came, they knew each other by now, and there was some exchange of what happened for them as well. Later it morphed into a shape where we were with the kids first to hear about their return, and then we called the parents in. We went around the circle again, and the initiates spoke about their experience for about five minutes each. In this way, the parents were able to witness at least a bit of the story in an environment that was empowering to the young people, and where they felt safe to speak from an honest place. Then we had the celebration feast.

When the probation officers heard about these meetings with the parents, they asked, "How in the world did you get those parents to come to your meetings? I'm constantly trying to get one of them to come to a meeting, and they never show up. And you often get both parents!"

We realized it had to do with the fact that these meetings were about something positive. They were about how the parents had done something right to raise a young person who was able to do something so amazing – something they could feel proud of, and perhaps even something that the parents weren't even sure that *they* could do themselves.

COUNCIL OF ELDERS

As we explored ways to support the incorporation phase of the vision fast, we researched what the early people did. When an initiate came back from the threshold time, he or she was greeted by the Council of Elders, which in some communities were the older men, and in some communities both men and women.

The Council of Elders asked the initiate to tell the story of what happened during those three or four days of being alone. As they listened, rather than looking for what was wrong, they asked, "What was it that Spirit wanted this person to know? What are the gifts that we see in this story to tell us about this young initiate?" They would sit around and just sort of bullshit about the story. "I wonder why this happened..."

We saw that the way in which they were listening to the story was not just for the young person, but for the whole community. Wisdom was listened for in the story. Wisdom was listened for about that person in particular, and how they could support the gifts of that person in the community. And it also was a story of wisdom for the community.

We decided to experiment with that idea, and we called a Council of Elders together. The council was made up of people who had been on a vision fast before. We came up with a series of questions that we put into the form of "the hero or heroine," and each elder asked a different question. "How did this hero prepare to go out on vision fast?" "When the hero got lonely, what did the hero do?" "What was the vision for the people that the hero brought back?" And the young person answered the question in third person, beginning with, "The hero..."

This helped to open up the story, because it's not always easy for young people to tell their story. By putting it in the third person, by talking about the archetypal "hero" instead of talking directly about themselves, they were able to see and tell their story more easily. They could also see that they were part of a bigger story.

We'd already heard the first telling of the story on the bus ride home. But we knew that for this ceremony to really be effective, it needed to be an integral part of the community, and not just held by us.

And as the elders came together to hold the initiates' stories, they also had an opportunity to rejuvenate their own experiences.

Our reputation continued to improve. Some people still thought we were pretty crazy, but they couldn't help but see that something positive was happening with the kids. Adults began asking us to take them out on a vision fast, and we couldn't say no. Before long, Rites of Passage developed into three branches: a youth program, an adult program, and a training program.

We called our training program Raccoon Lodge. The program prepared and encouraged other adults to bring this ceremony into their communities. We asked trainees to commit to at least a year – sometimes two years – of weekly meetings. They also participated in four vision fasts – two personal fasts and assisting in two fasts.

And of course, our trainees participated in the Council of Elders and were encouraged to keep nurturing those relationships.

We hired Marilyn Riley and Jack Crimmins to run the youth program. Marilyn is Steven's sister, and Jack is one of the young people who had first come through the program and stayed to volunteer. We watched him grow as he became an important, wonderful guide.

We often took two groups out a month. Marilyn and Jack took out the youth, and Steven and I ran the adult program. We'd all drive out to the desert together, and then take our groups up different canyons.

At the same time, we were working with our great and supportive Board of Directors, which included Frank Burton, Steven Blair, Timothy Garthwaite, Charlotte Horning, James Workman, and Howard and Sue Lamb. They were all part of a movement to bring earth-based ceremonies back into our culture, and they loved what we were doing. Now and then we went out and had a Board fast together.

Rites of Passage, Inc. was growing. We were no longer alone.

WE WERE NOT ALONE

In the early 1970s, the time was ripe for bringing earth-based wisdom back into our culture. It started emerging in diverse places. People sang "medicine songs" that came from many different traditions and different people. Some of them we could track to certain Native American communities, and some couldn't be traced. New songs were written. There was a mingling of diverse people and cultures.

There were a lot of gatherings at that time, and the one we really loved going to was Sun Bear's. Sun Bear was a prominent voice in the Native American movement. He was of Ojibwa descent, and he was the founder and Medicine Chief of The Bear Tribe Medicine Society. He was a big, wonderful, bear of a man with a great big heart and a whole lot of wisdom. We felt very connected to that wisdom, and he took us under his wing.

The Bear Tribe had large gatherings every year, where people of all ages and walks of life came together for ceremony and teaching. There were little kids running around, there were elders, there were people who were dressed really fancy, and there were people who were dressed funky. His gatherings were inclusive, and that's where we felt comfortable.

This was a time when we were all interconnected. There was excitement in the air. Things were happening all around us. There were a lot of other key people who were bringing new ways of thinking together.

Angeles Arrien was a cultural anthropologist, author, and President of the Foundation for Cross-Cultural Education and Research. Joan Halifax was the director of the Ojai Foundation for many years, and later would become a Buddhist monk. Bill Bridges was an author, speaker, and organizational consultant who used the rites of passage model to support corporate change. Michael Harner was an anthropologist and author who founded The Foundation for Shamanic Studies and the New Age practice of "Core Shamanism." Evelyn Eaton was a Canadian novelist who apprenticed extensively with Grandpa Raymond Stone before becoming a pipe holder and teacher of native shamanism. Jonathan Ledoux Swift Turtle was a Miwok elder who "adopted" us and taught us a lot about Native American protocol.

There were many others, as well. We were a loose network, getting to know and inspire each other. There was a weaving together of all of us who were trying to find new ways of returning earth-based ceremonies to the people. Many of these people became lifelong friends and colleagues.

One time there was a protest at the Diablo Canyon Nuclear Plant, south of the Bay Area. Many of us met there to do ceremony and try to bring healing. We invited the operator of the nuclear plant, and he and his young granddaughter joined us for a sunrise ceremony. We were all working together, trying to fight the good fight, build bridges, and honor the wisdom of the earth.

HYEMEYOHSTS STORM

It was probably in 1979, when Steven and I were out with a youth group and Ginnie was holding down the fort at home, that we first heard from Hyemeyohsts Storm. Storm was a "Metis," or mixed blood. His mother was Cheyenne, Sioux, and Irish-American, and his father was German. He had written *Seven Arrows* in 1972, a book that influenced Steven when he was first taking young people out to the desert. *Seven Arrows* introduced the Way of the Medicine Wheels, a Native American spiritual philosophy and earth science, to the modern world. It was the first time this teaching had been put into writing.

Steven had sent the manuscript of *The Book of the Vision Quest* to the publishers Harper & Row, asking if they would get it to Storm for a possible blurb for the back cover. While we were in the desert, Ginnie took a phone call that turned out to be Storm calling from Harper and Row, where he happened to be for a meeting. I still have the notes Ginnie scribbled while he was talking.

"You tell them that they have to come down here and meet me now. Right now," he said. "There are important things they need to know about publishing. There are important things they need to know about the work that they're doing. And I want to see them now."

She was excited, and when we came in the door after dropping the group off, she said, "I'll take care of Selene. You go down there and meet with him."

Storm lived in a little trailer near Santa Barbara, where he had been "hibernating" after *Seven Arrows* came out. Some people in the Native American community were very upset with him for what they saw as sharing their secrets, so he retreated for a while and began working on a new book.

Now he was feeling it was time to come out and get involved again. When we arrived at his trailer, he said, "What you're doing is important. You sit down here, and I'm going to teach you things you need to know."

And over the next 24 hours, he began to give us some of his teachings. It's hard to put into words the things he taught us that day and night. The medicine count, the medicine wheel … yet mostly it was his presence and how he interacted with the world around him, and with us.

This came at an important time for Steven and me. We were tired. We were both introverts, and we were constantly pushing boundaries, juggling a house full of people, trying to make time for our beloved family. We had a little girl running around, rightfully wanting our attention. We had high school kids in and out of the house, volunteers, group meetings, and networking with other people to develop new programs. It was a time of quickening, and we were exhausted.

There was also little time for Steven to write. He was a writer, and he had to write. We were going out at least once a month with a group after going into the schools, and then preparing them in our home. And we certainly weren't making money. We began saying to each other, "I'm not sure we can keep doing this." Then we looked into the eyes of a returning group, amazed at what had happened for them, and we said, "How can we not do it?"

After those first 24 hours with Storm, we came home dazed and excited. For the next two years, without any notice, Storm would appear suddenly at our door with his apprentice, Harley Swiftdeer, and his "army" – six or seven young trainees, some indigenous and some white, mostly in their twenties. They all moved into our house, and of course our house was already full. His "soldiers" slept out on the lawn, and Storm slept all day in our room while we worked.

When he woke up in the evening, he called to us and again said, "Okay now, sit down. I'm going to teach you." And he did. His teachings inspired us and gave us a new sense of understanding about what we were doing. We were reinvigorated.

Storm was very shamanic, and it was interesting to watch how he taught his apprentice, Harley Swiftdeer. He would have Swiftdeer go into a city dressed in his "Indian outfit" and convince people that he was a doctor, or a lawyer, or a beggar. It was shapeshifting. This teaching about what shapeshifting is, how we are always shifting shape, and how to take responsibility for that, we later wove into our teaching. A lot of those little things influenced us.

I can't remember all the things that he taught us. And it's not even that important. More importantly, he was one of the ones that helped us feel the way in which people who live close to the land interacted with it. When he saw a hawk, he'd stop, he'd send a prayer, and we saw the way in which nature was alive and teaching all the time. It wasn't just reading about ritual and ceremony, it was seeing him do it, and how he did it. We felt the authenticity of it, even though he was quite modern.

At the same time, he drove us crazy. He was a genius, as Steven was a genius, and they recognized each other. He honored Steven as a chief. And yet, in the end, what Storm wanted was for us to join his tribe. And in certain ways, he tried to separate Steven and me, because Steven was to be the chief, and I was the woman. I was supposed to do all the work and raise the money, and Steven was supposed to be the chief who did the teaching.

For us, of course, the root of our "magic" and teaching style came from the "we." We always said that "one plus one equals three." The two of us together were more than either of us alone, and Storm didn't understand that. He didn't really like it.

Even so, there was something magical about what we created with Storm for a while. And then we all moved on.

THE FOUR SHIELDS

There are Four Directions teachings all over the world. In almost any indigenous culture, you'll find some form of the Four Directions. All of them represent ways in which indigenous people were trying to put into words their understanding of the wisdom they saw in nature, and so, coming from observing the land, the teachings were very similar.

Storm's teaching was the "Four Shields," which originated in the Mayan culture of Central America and moved north to the Cheyenne people in the central plains of North America. The Four Shields is similar to many nature-based systems found around the world, tapping into the wisdom of the land. Aboriginal peoples found their orientation to the physical, psychological, mental, and spiritual aspects of the natural world, and their own maturing nature, in the teaching of the four directions.

In half an hour, Storm gave us the bare bones of the Four Shields. He taught us that these are not just abstract compass points, but rather living, breathing influences and expressions of life itself.

In a nutshell, the South represents summer, child, body, reactivity, instinct, innocence, and erotic love. The West represents fall, adolescence, psyche, introspection, memory, self-reflection, and self-love. The North represents winter, adult, mind, communication, manifestation, self-discipline, and love for others. The East represents spring, enlightenment, spirit, creativity, vision, renewal, mystery, and love of spirit.

The teaching is so seemingly simple, and yet so ultimately complex. For years we played with it, trying to understand it, using it with our people. We often sent them out on exercises to explore the Four Shields so we could learn more. We saw that nature itself evoked these shields in us, and by sending people out for a few hours specifically to experience certain aspects of nature, or a particular aspect of a shield, such as a sunrise or sunset, mountaintop or deep valley, they would learn more deeply about their own nature.

This became a basic teaching as we worked with trainees and prepared groups to go out. It helped them understand that the vision fast is about wholeness, not just about the "vision" of the East Shield. We need all the aspects of our nature, all the shields, in order to live a relatively healthy and balanced life.

In Steven's book, *The Four Shields,* he wrote that, "If there were a measure of 'mental health,' it would involve the ability of individuals to grow into the fullness of each season – that is, the ability to fully become, or enact, the contents of each shield."

Over time, we developed the Four Shields in our own way. We tried to make it fresh and interesting each time, despite giving that teaching so many times. We did this by not having any notes, learning new ways to speak of and understand this system, and sparking off each other. Steven said something new that made me think of something else, so it stayed alive. It was always an adventure, a creative discovery.

A CHOSEN DEATH

Ginnie and my father, Aldie, shared a story that when one of them died, the other one would follow. "If you die, I'll take our sailboat and just sail away," they said to each other. But at the very end, when my father was dying, he turned to her and said that she should find another man and marry again. He wanted to set her free from that story.

So here was Ginnie, six year's after Aldie's death, with these two conflicting stories. She truly believed that there was life after death, and she believed that she and Aldie still had work to do together. Even after living through most of the pain of losing him, she still felt called to "follow him." She had to figure out if it was the right thing to do. Finally, she decided it was.

This was the time when we asked Storm the question, "Do your people have a way of preparing to die?"

That night, Storm and his entourage had shown up at our house. We were sitting around the big table late into the night: Ginnie, Steven, Storm, and I with some of his "apprentices," and we said, "Ginnie wants to die a 'chosen death.' She wants to join her love, and she doesn't want to die from despair and unhappiness, but because it's time. Do your people have any wisdom about preparing for death?"

And he said, "Of course we do." That was the night Storm taught us about many of the ceremonies the people on his reservation used, both to prepare the dying person to leave the village, and to prepare the village for the loss. Some of these we later included as aspects of the vision fast: Decision Road, Death Lodge, Purpose Circle, and the Great Ballcourt.

These teachings originated with the Mayans and moved up to his reservation on the Central Plains. In short, when people in the village knew they were ready to die, they would step onto Decision Road to acknowledge that they were dying, enter a Death Lodge in the community where everyone could come and say goodbye, and then move to a Purpose Circle outside the village, where they would make it good with themselves and their God. There they would be left alone to die.

For the next year and a half, Ginnie began the Death Lodge work and the Purpose Circle work, visiting all her important people and letting them know what she was doing, hoping to make it good with them. We saw these teachings put into action.

Ginnie believed that, just like animals know how to die, when it's time, humans know how to die as well. So she set a date, sold her house and most of her belongings, and after a meal and prayers with close people, she went into her room to die.

But she didn't die. She had an experience of a hooded figure that pushed her back down and said, "You still have more to do."

"Okay," she said, "What more is there for me to do?" And so began her last year. She began thinking about people in rest homes who felt complete with their lives and were ready to die. She felt it was important that these people had the right to say, "My life has been good, and it's time for me to go."

She said, "Well, maybe it's good that I have to use pills to die, because it sets an example for other people." During that year, she found out the dosage, and in her last few weeks, she moved to North Carolina, where it was legal to commit suicide. She saw the pills as the tool that enabled her to have a "chosen death," and perhaps to be an example for others who felt complete in their life to do the same. To the very end, she was always the teacher.

We went out to North Carolina to be with her, some of her close family, and a few friends. She meditated twice a day, each time saying, "Okay God, not my will but thine. If I'm not supposed to do this, you need to show me." She kept 49 smooth, black pebbles in an earthen goblet, and every day for 49 days she buried another one in the earth. When all the pebbles were buried, it was time.

She had one last council the morning of her death. Each person, one at a time, had a chance to say last words to her. Two were angry, some were in tears, and she listened and thanked each one.

Ginnie was the last to speak. She looked at each person and said, "I love you," until she came back to herself, and said, "...and I love Aldie." Her death was quick and peaceful. It shook us – another death that shook us to the core.

Ginnie always believed that life was a preparation for the big transition into death. On some level, this was something she was preparing for her whole life. As we watched her put Storm's teachings into action, we began to see the relevance to people who were dying a symbolic death. We saw that the way to prepare for symbolic death was the same as Ginnie preparing for a physical death.

We asked, "What is a conscious, "chosen death" versus suicide? How do we recognize when it's time to die?" And by this, we meant not only physical death, but also symbolic death. How often do we hold onto a destructive relationship, afraid we can't make it on our own, or afraid of the unknown?

These questions deeply informed our work. We continued to explore ways to support people so that, when they're ready, they can say, "It's time to die from this relationship, situation, circumstance, or way of life. I'm going to do the work of dying to what was, and take the risk of stepping into a new unknown."

ANOTHER CHOSEN DEATH

Coming back home from North Carolina, we immediately had a group to take out. We had three good, solid trainees in base camp, so it was the first time that Steven and I were able to fast together. Usually one of us would stay and take care of Selene while the other would fast. But now, for the first time, we got to be buddies because we had trainees who Selene loved to take care of her.

The fourth day we came in with everybody else and immediately, of course, we were the guides and responsible for the group. We packed up and got everybody in the bus, drove through the night, and just before dawn we arrived in Novato. The group scattered.

Steven and I, finally, as dawn was just beginning to brighten the sky, fell into bed. We looked at each other and we both knew: it was time to move. It is a most amazing thing, this kind of knowing. It was as if Ginnie had left this "knowing" as a gift. We didn't say it then, but looking back on it, the gift she gave us was this: "There are times when you just know. And you trust, even though it's scary."

We looked at each other, and said, "It's time." A chosen death.

Steven asked, "Well, where shall we move to?" I said, "The Owens Valley." The Owens Valley was the place we loved. That's where our land and base camps were. It was one of those precious moments between us, a shared knowing.

We were ready to leave Novato for several reasons. Our house was overrun with people, and it was no longer healthy for our family. Selene was getting to an age where she didn't want to keep coming out to base camp with us. She loved it, and the desert is in her bones. But at the age of five, she wanted to have time with her friends.

Steven and I always said, "If something is not working for our family, then we change what we're doing." We no longer had enough time with our kids, and we didn't have enough quiet time with each other. The bottom line was our family and our love. It was becoming unhealthy.

Rites of Passage had been a part of Marin County for a long time. Our Board was incredible, but being a nonprofit organization made things a lot more complicated. Another reason for the move was that we'd had enough of nonprofits. We just wanted to be a mom-and-pop shop so we didn't need to tell anyone the "why" of our decisions. We wanted to make decisions on our own.

We also wanted to live closer to the land. We wanted to live the life we had always talked about, where we could drive for miles and not see a light. We wanted to actually live what we were trying to evoke in people by taking them out into the desert. By moving to Big Pine, we could create a way of doing this work that was much better for our family. We wouldn't have to do that long drive over the mountains. And we wouldn't have to answer to anyone else.

Because it wasn't easy to get to Big Pine, people had to really want to come, which was an important step in their commitment. We could prepare them in Big Pine, where base camp was no more than an hour away. We'd take them out, and Steven and I would take turns at base camp while they were fasting so that the other could be home with the kids. Halfway through, we'd switch.

We told our staff and our Board of Directors, "We want to give Rites of Passage away. We'll stay one year to transfer everything, so if some of you want it, it's yours. If you don't want it, that's okay, too. It's been good."

HANDING OVER RITES OF PASSAGE, INC.

That began a really full, crazy, stressful year. It was a hard year. There was a lot of tension around who would take over Rites of Passage. Our concern was about what we needed to do in order to "die cleanly" to this, and to leave behind something good for other people. Our Board, certainly, took on an important role in supporting the transition.

Before we left Marin County, we did a little more work with a private high school, Marin Academy. It's an unusual school where, toward the end of senior year, students can choose to do something meaningful for themselves from a variety of options.

One of those options was to join us for a vision fast as a way of marking their graduation. It came at the perfect moment for them. They'd finished their studies, but they hadn't yet had their official graduation ceremony. In between, they went out into the desert for three days and nights alone as a way of marking the end of childhood and stepping into adulthood. Most of them were literally leaving home after that, which definitely supported the ceremony.

We invited some of the teachers to come along with us so that when the kids went back, there was a teacher who understood what they'd just been through. The teachers said, "Well, wait a minute. We want to go out on our own vision fast. And then we want you to train us."

We understood that if we really wanted to do this well, we had to train people to take it back to their communities. It was important that the guides were teachers, pharmacists, ministers – regular people in the community who could support the returning initiates. So we took the teachers who wanted to go out, and we did some training with them.

The teachers at Marin Academy continue to offer the vision fast to their students today. I have occasionally run into their groups in Death Valley. Beautiful. Beau Leonhart and James Shipman, who carried on the tradition, began to offer "alumni quests" for past students, many of whom have their own children attending Marin Academy. Such a wonderful example of how to integrate community with this ceremony.

It wasn't until the very end of that year that it became clear who was going to take over Rites of Passage. It ended up being my sister

Jennifer, my father and Ginnie's youngest child, who was a beloved soul sister, and her partner Drew, who had been training with us for years and lived with us much of that time.

Jennifer and Drew ran Rites of Passage for about two years until Jennifer became pregnant, and they decided to move up to Oregon. It was then passed on to Miguel Batz and Mike Bodkin, both of whom had trained with us for many years. Eventually, Mike Bodkin made it his own and has been successfully running Rites of Passage, Inc. ever since.

We didn't take much in the move. I remember the last day, we were all packed up, and it was getting dark. There were meetings happening in the house below, and we had said goodbye to everybody. We took Selene, who was five, into the empty house and told her she could be the one who blew the candle out. We lit a candle in the empty living room and said a little prayer for the house and for our trip to our new home. Selene blew the candle out.

We got into the cars. Steven drove the U-Haul, and I drove our blue Ford pick-up truck with Selene going back and forth between us through the night. As the first light of morning was coming, we drove through the heavy fog over Tehachapi Pass and down into the Owens Valley. We arrived in Big Pine early that morning.

It was January, 1982, and it was warm! We parked outside and came into the empty house. It was the beginning of a new life.

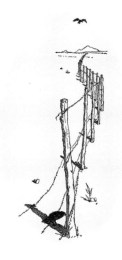

Part 3

The School of Lost Borders

EMPTY SPACE AND QUIET TIME

We hadn't realized that, in some important ways, we were not prepared for this new life. We had put all our energy into the enormous amount of work it took to hand over Rites of Passage, Inc. and to close things up in a good way. And then here we were in Big Pine, in the middle of winter in our small empty house, with a little wood-burning stove for the cold winter days. We knew nobody except our friend, Derham, who had helped us find our home in a little country town where, at that time, you weren't really accepted unless you'd lived here for years.

All of a sudden, from a very busy house with phones ringing and people coming through, we arrived at a place of almost complete quiet. Nevertheless, there was still a constant tension in me, expecting the phone to ring at any moment. I think I had an aspect of post-traumatic stress disorder (PTSD). It took me a long time to relax. We decided to have an unlisted phone number and do our work only by slow mail.

During our last year in Marin, Steven had written the first brochure for our new dream. Steven – brilliant Steven – came up with the name, "The School of Lost Borders."

The desert area around us was called, "The Land of Lost Borders" by the Paiute, because the borders became fuzzy and vanished into the desert. The name comes from both the land and the indigenous people here. It was the perfect name for what we were trying to do: get people to go past their usual borders.

In the early 1900s, a famous writer, Mary Austin, published two books about the area: *The Land of Little Rain* (1903) and *Lost Borders* (1909). In *Lost Borders* she wrote, "Ute, Paiute, Mojave, and Shoshone inhabit its frontiers, and as far into the heart of it as a man dare go. Not the law, but the land sets the limit. Desert is the name it wears upon the maps, but the Indian's is the better word."

We hoped and dreamed of The School of Lost Borders becoming mainly a training facility. It felt so important that as many kids as possible have a significant rites-of-passage experience, which meant training people to take it back into their own communities. This felt like a much more effective way of making an imprint on our culture than taking out one small group at a time.

But for the first year or two, we had no idea if anyone was going to come to our new school, and so we started looking for jobs. Steven looked for a teaching job (and was actually offered one near South Lake Tahoe), and I looked for waitress jobs. We trusted, but we knew that it might not happen, and if it didn't happen, we trusted that we'd find something else. If people didn't want what we had to offer, then we'd do something different. I'd inherited a little bit of money, which made it possible for us to get by very simply for about a year. It felt very much the same as it had when we started Rites of Passage, Inc.

At the same time, those years were so important because of their emptiness. Finally, Steven could write. And he did. Late into the night.

At his core, Steven was a writer and a poet – an incredibly creative man. Even if he was totally exhausted, the way he renewed himself was to write. He was constantly writing. He had ideas for books that just didn't end. He needed to write – not for the purpose of publishing, but to express himself. That was Steven.

I have at least four of his manuscripts that have never been published, as well as a lot of beautiful poetry. It was an important time for him, developing the writer and poet that was such a core part of who he was. He never felt that most of his books were good enough to publish, and his main focus at this time in his life was what would grow the work. He wrote *The Roaring of the Sacred River* as a potential training manual, and we talked a lot about how to best seed this ceremony back into our culture.

At the same time, here we were in the high desert that we loved so much, with a lot of time and space around us. We had time to deepen our understanding of the work we were doing, as well as deepen our relationship with the land.

So we explored the huge, accessible areas around us and enjoyed doing reconnaissance for new base camps. We went out on walks and asked, "What does it mean that nature is a mirror? How does it feel different if we go up to the top of a ridge and look out? What gets evoked in us when we go down by the water, or we take a night walk?"

We were constantly in the question: "How does the land communicate? How do we communicate with the land? In what ways do we hear the voice of the land, and what does it tell us?"

We also began the practice of going out fasting every year. Because we had kids at home, we couldn't go at the same time. So we put each other out, one at a time. Of course, that also deepened our understanding of the ceremony. It was not the fancy, idealistic view of what many thought it to be, but quite humbling. It deepened our sense of belonging. We recognized how it stripped away everything that wasn't essential, and how the land was always showing us parts of our self.

WORD BEGINS TO SPREAD

Because they couldn't call us, people really had to make an effort to come to the school. There was no such thing as email in the early 1980s, so they had to write letters to us, wait for a written response, and then find their own way here. They couldn't go online for road conditions at the last minute or text us that they were lost. It put a lot of responsibility and commitment on those people who wanted to come. Trainees had to be able to get themselves here.

We tried various ways of doing training over the years. We developed a two-week training program, where people came several days before an open fasting group, helped us put the group out, and then stayed several days afterwards for more training. They learned by actually doing it.

Other trainees came and stayed for a month or two. We sat together in our little backyard, Steven chipped arrow points as we talked, and we sent them out on the land every day. They found their own place to camp, scattered up along Big Pine Creek or under a nice, big pine tree somewhere. There wasn't any central camping place, and they liked the challenge of that. And we liked it, too.

It was a co-created experience, and that felt essential to the training. We didn't take care of them and tell them what to do. If they wanted to be ready to handle a group and whatever emergency might come up, then they needed to be self-directed and self-responsible.

Eventually, we discovered a piece of land up along Big Pine Creek at an elevation of about 7,000 feet. It had a private campground that was on a good chunk of wild land with the creek coming through it. The land was owned by Bud Hinds, a local who became a good friend. He let us use a beautiful part of it for our programs.

We built a sauna out there with the help of Elias Amidon. He trained extensively at the school and became a guide, along with his wife Rabia, and both were dear friends. He later became spiritual director (Pir) of the Sufi Way.

From then on, our groups began to camp up there. This also brought in the element – and the challenges – of community living.

Another thing we did when we came to Big Pine was deepen our involvement with the parents of youth who went out with us. We talked to the parents and sent them information before the youth arrived in Big Pine for their vision fast. Then we invited them to come down to Big Pine themselves when their young people came off the mountain.

A lot of the parents, and sometimes some of the siblings, came down to help celebrate what their son or daughter had done. They drove down or flew in, and we met with them separately the morning before the Elder's Council. Then we invited them to join the Council of Elders to hear the full stories of their sons or daughters as they were told for the first time.

After we mirrored a story, we invited the parents to speak about how they witnessed this moment. As we had done at Rites of Passage, Inc., we encouraged them to find some new privilege, responsibility, or family heirloom they could give to their child to acknowledge and honor the young person's step into adulthood.

Slowly, more people began to hear about and come to The School of Lost Borders. And then word really began to spread. We had groups come in from Europe. Colleges began to send groups of students. Joan Halifax, who was director of the Ojai Foundation at the time, began to bring a group every year. Almost every time she brought a group, she also went out to fast. Toward the end, she began her path more deeply into the Buddhist faith and eventually became a Buddhist monk

After a while, our social needs were more than taken care of by the groups that came through. Yet, for most of the people who did come, and who we loved, we were always the trainers. We had a few important, really close people who we saw now and then, but there was also a kind of loneliness. It was a loneliness that came from being put up on a pedestal, and then constantly having people try to take you down.

I remember a fast one year, when it came up painfully for me that I felt people loved me, but they didn't actually see me. What they loved was what I gave them. I had to really adjust myself to saying, "Well, they love parts of me, and who I am to them is also a true part of me."

There were a few people from Big Pine who came out with us, but mostly we protected our identity in town. We wanted to just be neighbors. Obviously, our people were coming through, staying in the hotels and buying gas and things from the store. Our work was supporting the town.

Sometimes people in town asked our people, "What are you doing here?" We warned our people to be careful how they talked about it. When people asked us directly, we said, "We're taking them to the mountains for a nature experience."

There was a lot of gossip about us. We heard some people say, "They're the ones that have all those intelligent people coming through." Another story was that we were "sorcerers." Gossip. We had a few friends who knew more about us, such as Bobby and Margie, who lived across the street. Back then, it was a pretty conservative place, and we just wanted to find common ground with people. We were mostly able to protect our identity and just be neighbors.

Steven's son, Christian, was on the football team at Big Pine High School, which is a very important role in a small community. We went to the football games and cheered with our neighbors. Selene did well in school, and everybody loved her, so they figured her parents must be OK, too.

Steven was a beloved varsity and junior varsity basketball coach at the high school, and he sometimes coached elementary students too. When Selene was in fourth grade, her teacher, Bill Todd, who later became a good friend, invited Steven to teach a survival arts class (fire-making, flint-knapping, basket-weaving, native foods, etc.) at Big Pine Elementary School.

Fourth grade is when the school curriculum introduces Native American studies. Big Pine has a Paiute reservation, as every little town up and down the valley has, and a large Paiute-Shoshone population that lives on the reservation. For years, Steven taught that class once a week during the winter, and it made a big impact on the kids, I think, especially the young Paiute and Shoshone students, who found pride in their indigenous legacy. Bill Todd said that their grades went up after Steven came in to teach.

They loved him. And so did the community. If the conversation got to politics, religion, or certain topics that might cause tension, we sought common ground: love for family, love of the land, and the belief that, if a neighbor is in trouble, you are there to help. It doesn't matter what your religion is, or what your politics are. We're neighbors. That's fundamental. That was a very beautiful way of life.

EXCITEMENT AND DREAD

Soon we got too busy again. It got to the point where one group left and another group arrived the next morning. We rarely had a day to ourselves without someone other than family in our home.

There were times when I was exhausted. There were times that were incredibly stressful. There were often times when we mirrored 10 or 11 stories a day. All we could do was let go of one, listen to the next, and let go of that. It couldn't stick. We had to keep going. We had to keep showing up for the next group.

That was our life. Because of the kind of people we were, work was not separate from our personal life. Over a two-year period, we counted how many days we had the house to ourselves with just our family. One year it was one day. The next year it was two days.

We felt ambivalent about all of it. Yes, we were doing the work that felt like ours to do, and it was meaningful. Yet, there was a way in which we dreaded showing up for the next meeting. There was both excitement and dread. Did we look forward to the next group coming? Not really. Did we come to love the people in every group? Absolutely. Could I remember their stories a week later? Mostly no. Could I remember all the faces a month later? Not too many. Even though I genuinely came to love them, and I loved listening to their stories, did I forget some of them? Yes I did.

I had to be gentle with myself. We were running a business with people coming in and out and all the demands of office work. And we had our family life. There were five of us living in this little house. We had two big teenage boys – Christian and his friend, Roger, who came to live with us – and our little Selene. And Steven and I had our relationship. Working together can be a joy. But there's also tension around it sometimes.

This was all mixed together. Sometimes there were mornings when Steven and I were angry at each other, and we had to pull it together to show up for the group. Get in the car, go up to the campground, sit down, meet for God knows how many hours. We just had to let it go so we could show up. And when we came home again, we usually looked at each other and said, "Boy, that was a silly thing we were angry about this morning."

Doing the work itself made the world bigger. Sometimes our little stuff was just a result of the tension and stress. But not always. There were certainly times when we were working things out as a couple. There was that dance: when did we keep communicating and working through these things, and when did we need to pull it together, open the door and greet the people who were there, and set our stuff aside until later?

On one hand, it was a good thing, because the School was really happening. But on the other hand, we found ourselves in the same situation we'd left in Novato. Our house was always full, and it wasn't good for our family. We felt like the kids were suffering again.

So we made a commitment to take three months off every winter. We had to create more balance in our lives, and we urgently needed to take those three months off when we had no group work. It was such a relief when November finally came.

In those winter months, I did bookkeeping and taxes, applied for permits and insurance, and signed people up for the next year's programs. It was a chance to catch up on all the office work. Steven had his writing and his involvement with the high school and elementary school. And most importantly, we had time for each other and with our kids. The winters were our time.

At one point I realized that, from that first day of November, I was already thinking, "Oh my God, I'm going to have to start doing it all over again in February." After a couple of winters like that, I realized that my time off was being destroyed by the dread of what was going to happen again in three months. I took it out on fast one year, and it became clear I had to learn the wonderful lesson of "living in the moment." Everything got a little better after that.

DERHAM AND ENID

We had three important teachers once we moved to Big Pine. The first was our neighbor, Derham Giuliani, who lived in a little room behind us when he wasn't out on the land. The second was Enid Larsen, who also lived behind us and from whom we rented our house. The third was Grandpa Raymond Stone, the Paiute Elder of the Valley.

We first met Derham a few years before we moved to Big Pine, when we brought a group of young people from the Bay Area into the Saline Valley. He was caretaking an old miner's cabin. Early each morning, he went out to where hundreds of migrating Monarch butterflies were overnighting in the trees and marked the wing of each one with a dot of white correction fluid – the kind used for typing. This would tell people who were studying the migration further north or south that the monarchs had come through the Saline Valley.

We immediately realized that this was an amazing man. Very simple, very shy. Not comfortable around people. Except that he liked what we were doing, and he liked people who loved the desert.

The night we met him, Selene had developed a bad case of the croup. Her cough sounded terrible. So here we were, out in the middle of nowhere with a very sick baby, and we were getting ready to take a large group of kids up a canyon into the mountains.

We went to the old miner's shack and Steven said, "Derham, our baby's sick, and I have to take a group of kids up into the mountains. Will you take my wife and baby to the hospital?"

Immediately, he said, "Of course." It was quite a drive to Bishop – especially in the winter, on a long, winding, unplowed dirt road. When we got inside the hospital, I could tell he was really uncomfortable, a bit like a wild animal suddenly enclosed. I said, "Derham, it's okay. Why don't you go outside?" But he waited for us in the waiting room, and drove us back. After that, he became an important friend who helped us often over the years.

Derham had never married, and he had very few "friends," although quite a few people knew him. He chose not to go to college or university, because he wanted to learn from the land itself. He was a highly respected entomologist and animal behaviorist, and he was often hired by professors to do their field work. We thought he was a certified genius.

Sometimes he helped us get a group out to base camp with his truck. He would stay overnight and show the people how to pick up stones to find scorpions underneath. He would tell us stories about the animals out there, and the fascinating world under our feet. We all learned a lot from him.

Derham was the most indigenous white person we had ever known. His home was in the desert and mountains, where he spent most of his time. He had very little money, rarely washed his clothes, lived in one tiny room, slept on a mattress on the floor, and raised Ringtail Cats in his room and the adjacent Quonset hut. He liked what we were doing. He especially loved that we took our baby into the wild, carrying her on our backs up steep canyons and sleeping on the ground.

When we began looking for a place to live in the Owens Valley, Derham told us that his landlady had a house for rent in Big Pine. Both the house and its owner, Enid Larson, were simple and great for us, so we became neighbors.

Derham had a lot of insight about our work. He understood it in ways that few others did. It was always fun when he came to the back fence, or the front door at night, to ask about our current group. He saw how taking people back to their natural habitat brought out different qualities that couldn't be accessed in the civilized world, and he saw how it changed them.

One day he decided he wanted to experience the vision fast himself, and we were curious: here was a man completely comfortable in nature, unafraid and very used to being alone for long periods of time. What would it be like for him? We sat with him and asked him what his "intent" was that he would take into the ceremony.

He said, "Here I am, President of the Pantheist Society, and I absolutely think that everything is sacred and 'godlike' except...I'm not sure if humans are. How could I be President of the Pantheist Society if I don't think there is anything sacred about human beings?"

So he went out to ask. We loved it. Here was an extremely brilliant, rational man, who had been turned mystic by being on the land so much. He began to have experiences that he just didn't understand, that could only be called "mystery."

He went out buddying with Steven on his annual personal fast. And he had an experience that blew him away, and brought back the message that although he may not like most humans, and rarely trusted them, they too were godlike and sacred.

On our drive back home from the fast, he had to stop and walk along the top of a thin railing to see if his balance was better after fasting. He walked it without a slip. Derham had such a brilliant mind. His need to prove everything was part of his delight.

Our landlady, Enid Larson, lived in a small house behind ours on the property we shared with Derham. She was a small, seemingly fragile older woman born to a ranching family in the Valley in the early 1900s. She was all fire and strength, with a fierce passion for nature and beauty.

The Forestry Service knew Enid well. She often stormed into their office, furious about some decision they were trying to make that she felt jeopardized the Valley. Eventually, they learned to come to her first to ask her opinion. She was a biologist and retired biology teacher who never married, and whose students from years before still came to visit her. She received her PhD from Berkeley during the Great Depression, and she still buried emergency money in her backyard, a response she had after finding herself penniless one day wandering Berkeley.

Enid was a world expert on the Merriam's Chipmunk. She had spent thousands of hours studying them from Western California, to Baja, to the White Mountains. I tried to visit her most days and became what you might call her secretary, helping her finish her long research manuscript, *Merriam's Chipmunk on Palo Escrito: The Life History and Naturalistic Behavior,* which is now at the Academy of Science in San Francisco. I often drove her up into the White Mountains to help her count the chipmunks and note what they were eating.

Enid grew up in the Valley and lived most of her life here, so we learned a lot about its history and natural history from her. She had a lot of stories and pictures about what the Valley used to look like. She taught us about its vegetation and wildlife, and she told us about wonderful places to go and explore. Many of those became our base camps.

Every month, Enid put out the *Waucoba News*. Waucoba is the name of a mountain here, and the newsletter was full of articles about the biology of the Valley. A couple of hundred people looked forward to getting it each month. I helped her type it up, print it out, and distribute it.

The Paiute people loved Enid, and she really cared about and respected them. She was a real mentor for me, and I spent quite a bit of time with her, especially as she became more and more physically weak in the ten years we knew her.

GRANDPA RAYMOND STONE

Hyemeyohsts Storm had come along at a key moment in our lives. There's no question that Ginnie was foundational to our work. But Grandpa Raymond Stone was the one who taught us about the indigenous way of perceiving the world like no one else.

When we first moved to Big Pine, we asked Jonathan Ledoux Swift Turtle, a Miwok elder and friend, the best way to let the native people know that we were here. He told us that we needed to take a gift to the elder of the Valley, and to ask permission to use the land.

We discovered that the Paiute elder, Grandpa Raymond Stone, actually lived here in Big Pine. We found out where he lived and took a blanket and some food over to him. He lived in a little house at the edge of the reservation, with a sweat lodge in the backyard, where he and his wife raised ten children.

Grandpa Raymond came out and sat with us. We told him that we had just moved here, and we told him about the work we were doing. We said that we didn't want to intrude on his territory, but we wanted to ask permission to do our work and take people into these mountains.

He said, "You do good work. You need to do that work for your people." He was very generous and supportive. He let us know that it would not be okay to do a sweat lodge, but that we could certainly do our work, and take them into the mountains. We asked him if we could bring our people to see him now and then, and to ask questions, and he agreed. This began another very important relationship for us.

Grandpa Raymond was the real thing. He had been taught by his father, who had been taught by his father. He was, as his father was, an "Indian doctor," which meant that he did healing in his sweat lodge, but he never called himself a healer. He would say that he did not do the healing, but that spirit worked through him. He said that, in order for there to be any healing, the person who wanted to be healed had to come halfway. If they were willing to come halfway, then he would take them into his lodge and he would call in the spirits and find out how to do the healing.

He studied with his father for many years before being ready to go up on the mountain to claim himself a sweat lodge leader. The act of doing the ceremony marked the new role. He would say that nothing in particular had to happen, but the act of doing the ceremony marked the new role, which he then came back and took on formally.

He also did this when he took on his spirit helpers. For years he would develop a relationship with, for example, Hummingbird, calling them into his lodge to help him with healing, asking them how to use them, and only after he had a deep relationship with the animal or spirit, did he go out to fast and claim the helper's medicine. Just as we had come to understand in our own work, he also saw the vision fast ceremony as confirmatory, helping us to understand this aspect even more deeply.

When Grandpa originally fasted for his sweat lodge, the spirits came to him and told him that he was to let in anyone who came to the door of his sweat lodge. We saw the pain in him over the years, when some of his own people were angry with him for allowing whites to come into his lodge. They were hard on him about that, so he would shut his lodge down. He'd pace and he'd be so sad, and he wouldn't know what to do, and finally, it always ended the same, he'd remember what he was shown on that fast. "If someone comes to the door of the lodge and asks, you let them in." So he'd open his lodge back up. But the Paiute people began to come less and less often, even as more and more people came from outside the Valley to sweat with him.

Sometimes he still put people out on the mountain, or more often they went without food and water in the sweat lodge for four days and nights over a period of a year, usually two days at a time. He talked with them beforehand about the intent they brought to the ceremony. Every day he would go into the lodge with them and lie down, sometimes falling asleep. When he woke up he asked, "Who's coming to you?" Then he'd go back home a few steps away and watch TV.

Grandpa's relationship with spirit was such a teaching for us. Spirit was not something separate from the animal or plant or person. Spirit was in and of everything, and so everything is respected and honored. If he asked a question of Bear or Hummingbird or his Grandmother who had died, he completely acted on their response.

"What spirit says is what I do." No question. That was it. Absolute integrity.

Now and then, he asked me to be the "interpreter" in his lodge, which meant that if he wanted to speak with Bear, he asked me to ask Bear the questions, and I was to tell him what Bear said. This took an enormous amount of trust for me to get out of the way and listen for what instantly came. This was a big deepening in my relationship with the land around me, and with life itself.

Having the opportunity to practice asking and listening, and to do it with someone who immediately took whatever "Bear says" as absolute and used it in a good way, really helped me trust that inborn ability to communicate without the mind. It taught me to trust that, if I truly listened deeply to a story without trying to do anything with it, and if I just opened my mouth and caught the first few thoughts that came through about the story, then the rest would come.

Mirroring at its best is getting out of the way and letting whatever it is that Spirit wants that person to know, be heard and seen. I certainly can't always do that. I get in my own way, but Grandpa was giving me that opportunity. He taught me a lot about how to trust that more.

Every now and then, we went over to just sit with Grandpa and talk. He called it bullshitting. We asked him questions. We laughed together. We began to bring our groups to him to ask questions. One of the people asked, "Well, Grandpa, how do you pray?" And Grandpa laughed. "You've been sitting here, bullshitting with me for 20 minutes, and you don't think you know how to pray? That's all you do. You just bullshit! You know, you just have to ask! If you don't ask, you're not going to get any answers, so you just start talking!" It was so simple, and so true. That kind of wisdom was a blessing for us all.

We also began to bring our groups to Grandpa for a sweat lodge after they came off their fast, and it was a wonderful closing to their ceremony. Unfortunately, the others who came to his lodge, who were mostly white people, began to say things to our people like, "Oh, you had water while fasting! That's easy. You didn't have a real Native American shaman put you out on the mountain."

Those kinds of comments demeaned the experience for our people. They'd just come off the mountain, done a very strong ceremony, and immediately had to face criticism. It began to be more and more uncomfortable, and they didn't need that. So we stopped bringing them to the sweat lodge.

Grandpa finally said to us, "Either you bring your people here and I prepare them and put them out my way, or you go and do it your way." And so, we parted ways, although we never stopped feeling his support for us and our work.

Grandpa Raymond was well respected from far distances. Native Americans as well as white people knew about him. He was simple and unassuming, yet he had a wonderful sense of humor. He was wise, kind, and strong. He was a deeply devoted man. When he died, there was a long caravan of cars, and people who came from many places. He was very important to us, and he was well loved by many.

SELF-GENERATED CEREMONY

People sometimes said, "There's a Navajo tradition of the Vision Quest." Or, "There's the traditional Cheyenne ceremony, or the Zulu way." But we discovered that the medicine person who guided the ceremony at any given time in the history of the tribe put different clothes on the bare bones of that tradition's ceremony to make it relevant to the needs of the community at that time.

Every initiate needed something that was going to push him to the edge and deepen the qualities in the individual that the whole community needed to stay healthy. For some tribes, the "ordeal" was to hunt and kill an animal, perhaps barehanded. That bravery and skill ensured food for the people.

We felt it was important to keep asking ourselves, "What are the bare bones of the ceremony that don't change? And what are the different clothes it can wear to support people in the givens of their world today?"

We realized that when communities still lived close to the land, walking on the earth was no big deal. They had that relationship with the natural world all the time. But staying in one place, in one circle, like with some ceremonial traditions, might have pushed the edges for them, or staying awake all four nights. For some tribes, going without food was not unusual. They went without food quite often if there was a hard year or a cold winter – but going without water pushed them to the edge.

So we asked ourselves, "What pushes people today? What qualities might the ceremony contain that support the individual in dealing with the truth of the world they will return to?"

We knew that going without food was a big edge for our culture. But going without water for four days in these modern times could be dangerous. If one goes without water, the toxins that are inevitably in our bodies these days have no way of getting out, and people can become very sick. So drinking lots of water to "clean out" felt more meaningful.

And instead of telling people, "You have to stay in one circle the whole time," we said, "Find your place within a mile or so of base camp so you can get back if you need help. And during those days, you can roam." We knew that this only increased the risk, and yet it felt so important that modern people have the experience of walking on the land, developing a relationship with it, and engaging with it, rather than staying in one place. If it was, for some reason, meaningful for them to stay in a circle, then they could trust that, too.

We also felt that modern people, in order to deal with the challenges of our world today, needed to learn how *not* to give their power away to teachers, leaders, or other authority figures who "knew better," but to learn how to trust their own nature and wisdom, and to reclaim their direct relationship with Spirit or God. They needed to learn how to create meaning for themselves, even though, as Ginnie often said, "It's far more difficult to surrender to our own knowing than to someone else's."

And so, self-generated ritual or ceremony became a key teaching that we offered before they went out. They could use it, or not use it. If there was an understanding that felt really strong, and they wanted to mark it when they were out there, we gave them some tools to do that.

We offered them the bare bones and said that they could create their own ceremony, using their own religion, their own spiritual faith, their cultural symbols and personal symbols, their own actions, their own words. It was beautiful to watch how easily and naturally people did this. They created ceremonies for themselves that were so much richer than anything we ever could have offered them.

We often talked with young people about finding a time during their three-day solo for cutting, burying, burning, or taking some other action that marked severing from their parents and their relationship with them as children. They came up with some beautiful ceremonies. Young people love ceremony, and they yearn for it in their lives. Truth is, we all yearn for it.

For one young woman, dealing with her upbringing as a Mormon was an important step in making that passage cleanly. We've had a lot of people fast with us who are Mormon, and who brought and used their own beautiful symbols. This young woman, however, knew she had to sever from that religion in order to find her own spiritual meaning.

She didn't know if Mormonism was her way or not, and she knew that she had to first let go of it before she could reclaim it as her own. She had already done a ceremony to sever from her mother and father, but this ceremony was much more difficult for her. She decided to go up to the top of a ridge and find a big rock. Her idea was that she would first let the place know what she was marking, and then throw her rock over the cliff as hard as she could.

She was terrified. Absolutely terrified. The way she'd been taught was, that if you let go of Mormonism, you will go into a place of nothingness. She was really afraid that when she threw that rock, she might go into a place of void.

Finally she said a prayer, took the rock, and threw it off the cliff. As she did, she felt an urge to turn and look down the canyon. There she saw Jesus, still with her. The message she heard was, "I will never leave you. No matter where you go, I will always be with you."

How rich we are innately, that we have this understanding about how to make meaningful ceremony. And how powerful it is when we give that back to people. Realizing this felt like a real key. In today's modern culture, we are often missing this piece – our human need to mark, not just with our mind and psyche, but with our whole being, the completions, new beginnings, and important moments of our lives.

ARE YOU SUICIDAL?

We began to see the importance of using the Four Shields as a way to listen to people we were preparing and screening. In the south, we asked, "Are they able to be reactive? Can they be emotional? Are they in their bodies?" In the west, "Are they able to be self-reflective, to access their inner world and express their feelings?" In the north, "Are they able to be responsible? Are they taking care of their equipment? Will they, if there's a storm, be able to take care of themselves?" And in the east, "Do we see a connection with their spiritual nature?"

If we didn't see all Four Shields activated in people, we knew they could be a liability when they hit uncomfortable times on solo. We'd seen it happen before. So we took that person aside and said, without judgment, "We know what it takes to get through this, and we are worried because we see (or don't see) .... We need you to convince us that you can really take care of yourself." It was not uncommon for someone to break into tears, relieved, and admit that they didn't feel ready. We invited them to stay at base camp with us and go out on walks each day instead.

I remember one beautiful middle aged man who, during the screening, showed a lot of dark, a lot of shadow, and admitted to having been suicidal. He was a very quiet, big-hearted person, but with lots of darkness. He was gay, which was part of the burden he carried. Life had been difficult for him in a lot of ways.

So we took him aside and said, "There's a lot of shadow in your life, and a lot of reason for there to be shadow. And you've talked about being suicidal, which in and of itself isn't necessarily a danger sign. We just wanted to check with you. We worry how you'll be when you're alone and difficult feelings come up."

He began to tell us about the other side of his life: he worked at a place for the criminally insane, people who had been arrested and were mentally unstable. He loved these people. His job was to counsel them. He told us that he had let these men know that he was going out on vision fast, and he wanted them to know what he was going to do.

"If any of you want me to pray anything for you, write it down on a little piece of paper and give it to me." His plan was that on the fourth day of his fast he was going to find a high ridge, and one by one he was going to read the prayers and let them blow away in the wind. In his story, we heard the love and care that he had for these men. And it became clear that he was more than fine. He brought some big teaching for all of us.

We realized that being suicidal wasn't necessarily a sign that they would be a danger to themselves. But we also learned that, if we had any feeling that someone might be suicidal, we had to talk with them about it. We simply asked, "Are you suicidal?" And if they were, they told us. We knew, from our training, experience, and work in our early days together at Suicide Prevention, that if they could talk about it, it immediately reduced their liability.

I remember one morning we were sending a group of young people out, and a young girl came up to me crying and crying. She said, "I was afraid to tell you, I've tried to commit suicide a couple of times, and I'm really afraid that I'm going to commit suicide out there. I feel like I don't have any control over it."

If this had been a different "therapeutic setting," I might have sat her down and talked with her. Instead, I found myself saying, "Can you promise me that, if for any reason you feel like you're going to hurt yourself out there, you'll come in first? Can you promise me that you'll come back?"

She said, "Oh yes, thank you! Thank you! That helps me! I might not be able to trust myself, but I know I can make that promise to you."

"Great," I said. "Then go out, and be with Death in some way. See if you can find out more about your relationship with Death."

The story she brought back was mind-blowing. She did a ceremony with Death. She called in Death by carving a "death stick," made a little fire, and tried to burn her relationship with Death. She said, "If I can just burn it, then it'll never plague me again." But it didn't burn. Each time she put a stick in the fire, it went out. She could not get rid of her relationship with Death.

Instead, she was shown by the fire that Death will always be with her, and that she can forge a different relationship with it. Death became her ally in living fully, rather than her enemy. Very beautiful

THE POWER OF STORIES

As we explored the practice of mirroring, we realized that we needed to create opportunities for our trainees to get experience working with the story of a returning faster. We met with them in the mornings and sent them out with an exercise in nature for two or three hours in the afternoons. Each one came back with a story, and they practiced mirroring with each other.

As we did that, we began to see how much could happen just by sending people out for an hour or two. We saw how deeply people could go in a very short amount of time, just by marking the gateways and observing the same taboos that were used in the vision fast ceremony — no company, no food, no artificial shelter.

This practice evolved into what Steven called "field therapy." We began to offer week-long seminars on a certain theme, and each afternoon we sent people out on ceremonial solo time for a few hours. We realized how important this was in helping them integrate the vision fast experiences into their lives, weaving the worlds together. It also was a great way to teach the Four Shields.

The Four Shields teaching seemed so simple, and yet the more we got into it, the more complex it became. The first time Steven tried to write a book about the Four Shields, we looked at each other and said, "It's too complex for us right now. It has to get simple again."

We were learning so much about this earth-based psychology so quickly by sending people out on the land in ways that we knew would evoke the different shields. We saw how the land so beautifully reflected all the different aspects of our own nature by watching a sunrise, taking a night walk, sitting by the river. The stories that the trainees brought back were teaching us, as much as anyone, about the depth and the wisdom contained in the Four Shields of our own human nature.

As Steven and I had more time to get out on the land ourselves, we recognized how much the land reflected where we were at any given time in our lives. And at the same time, we saw how much we mirrored the land. It went both ways. When the wind is blowing hard in Death Valley in the spring, it shakes everything up inside as well as out. When we climb to the top of a ridge and look out, a different aspect of ourselves is brought out than when we walked down deep into a dark canyon. And what is it that attracts us to a particular place on a particular day or time in our life? We could see that reciprocal relationship between the land and us, and we began to see more and more what it meant in terms of how to mirror a story.

I remember one woman – she was a housewife, a wonderful woman, and really excited about going out to do the vision fast. Her way of getting ready and avoiding her fear was to stay in her North Shield and be very practical. She'd bought all the right equipment, and she learned as much as she could about the practical side of it. But we could see, as we were preparing her, that this was a way of not dealing with the fear. We asked, "Don't you have any fear?"

"No, no!" she said. "I'm excited! I'm all ready! I've got it together!" We let her know that what was waiting out there for her was her life, and if she talked about what was up in her life, it would help her prepare. She continued to say everything was fine.

She went through the threshold circle in the morning and walked to the place she'd picked in this beautiful little canyon that wasn't very far away. But that afternoon, she came back in, and she was just enraged, sobbing and crying. "That canyon! That canyon!" she said. "There's been war in that canyon! There's violence in that canyon! That's a terrible canyon! And I wasn't sure you'd be here. I thought you might have left!"

We had come to trust that the ceremony always takes us where the healing is, and that the land mirrors what's really happening in us. We sat her down and she began to talk about violent times in her life that haunted her, and that she had tried to avoid thinking about because they were too painful. And she told us about all the people who had abandoned her when things were difficult.

Another woman came out with us after being in a shamanic workshop. She had met spirit helpers who told her she needed to go on a vision fast. She needed to feel "at one with the earth" and dance with the Grandmothers.

"You know, that's fine," we said. "But what you're going to meet out there is your life. Do you want to talk about what's happening in your life?"

"No, no, no," she said. "That has nothing to do with why I'm here! I'm here to do these ceremonies."

"Well," we said, "we have some concerns about you then. If you can't talk about your life here before you go out, we're afraid that you're going to meet it out there, and we're not sure how you'll be able to handle it." She said, "I'm fine. It has nothing to do with my life at home."

We decided to watch her carefully, and we had her promise that she'd stay just around the corner not too far away. On the afternoon of the second day, here she came, crying, and so angry with us. "You've tricked me! This is not what is supposed to happen!" All she'd been able to do was to lie under her tarp for two days. She couldn't leave, she couldn't take walks, and she couldn't do her ceremonies. She just lay there with all the feelings and thoughts about what was happening in her life that she was so unhappy about.

And bless her, she decided to come in and stay the rest of her solo time at base camp. Every afternoon she went out on a walk, and she came back and talked with us about what was coming up. When the group returned and we started doing stories, we treated her story as we did all the others. When her turn came, she told the real story. She told the unhappy story of her home life. It was very healing for her, and it was the beginning of a quest to find the help she needed.

There was a man who came out with us who'd been an amazing therapist for the whole of his adult life. He was a really good therapist. He said, "I've had it. I'm 70 years old, and the work is just getting to be too much. I'm tired, and I want to mark my retirement."
Of course, he hadn't retired yet. He was still seeing his patients. But he insisted, "I'm ready."

When he came back from the fast, his story said nothing about retirement. Instead it was full of the love he had for the people, and how much his work was meaningful for him. I kept listening for something in the story that said, "It's time to retire." But nothing in the story said that.

So we gave him the truth of what the land had shown him. That next year turned out to be a really important year of saying goodbye, of closing up his practice, of dying to what was. He needed that time to do the work of letting go of something that was important to him and had been deeply meaningful to him. A year later he returned and said, "Okay. Now I'm ready." And he went out to mark his retirement, which he then did beautifully.

These examples continued to show us that the ceremony always takes people right where they need to go, although not necessarily where they *want* to go. And if we could help them catch that, it led them toward healing.

Certainly as guides, we could never really know what people needed. We continued to recognize, more and more, that our role was not to counsel people, not to tell them what to do, but to hold a safe space for them to do their own ceremony. Our role was to receive them on the other side with love, without judgment. We were there to hear and witness the stories in such a way that they could understand for themselves what the message was for them.

THERAPEUTIC, BUT NOT THERAPY

When Joan Halifax first began bringing groups to us, she did a wonderful job of preparing them first. She took them into a sweat lodge, did her incredible deep work with them, and then brought them to us to take out on fast. We told Joan, "You can't bring more than 12 people at a time. More than that is too risky."

But one time, she showed up with 20 people. They had just been through a very intense week with her and had many new self-insights. We realized, as we listened to them, how all this new material was shaking them up. And in addition to the size of the group, it made them more of a liability.

So we went to Grandpa Raymond, and said, "Grandpa, what are we going to do? All these people, they have all this new stuff, and we're afraid that if we ask them to have an intent, it will be too much." He said, "You tell them all that they're going out there to pray for strength, wisdom, and understanding. Period."

This helped us understand even more deeply that preparation for this ceremony was not a time to "dig deeper" and shake new things up. Rather, it was confirmatory in nature. First, it brings something to a close. And second, it opens the initiate to what can grow out of that ending. So confirming where they were in the moment was the best way for them to get where they wanted to go. It showed us, once again, that the work might be therapeutic for some, but it was not "therapy."

Over the years, we saw many people come out who had been in therapy for a long time. They so deeply understood their traumatic experiences. They'd done the therapy, they had the understanding, and yet they felt like they still couldn't let it go. It was still plaguing them.

So we said, "Good. Go out there to formally mark that healing has been done around this traumatic event. You can't make the event go away, but your relationship with that event is new. It is a more healed relationship." This brought the finishing piece to their work. They were able to mark an ending with their whole being, not just the head and heart. Once the ceremony was enacted, there was no going back. It was like marking the passage from childhood to adulthood.

One woman came who had been divorced ten years before. She had been to therapy, and she absolutely knew that there was no way that the relationship was ever going to be there again. Yet, she kept feeling like she was always looking backwards. What she really wanted was to get married and move to Alaska. That was her dream. But she still felt somehow bound by that old relationship.

So we said, "Okay, good intent. You're going out there to formally confirm that marriage is dead. That it's done. Then you can turn and look forward."

She had a wonderful time, a wonderful four days. She didn't think a lot about her ex-husband, she didn't think a lot about the old relationship, and yet she carried through her solo time the intent that her old life was coming to completion. She did some simple ceremonies around that, and this gave room during most of her fast for dreaming into the future.

About a year later, she wrote to us and said, "It was so amazing. I came back into my life and suddenly, I was free. I was no longer looking behind me." In that year since her vision fast, she had re-married and moved to Alaska. The more we learned about this, the better we got at being able to help people put words to their intent.

The people who often had the most trouble understanding the difference between therapy and mirroring were therapists themselves. The range of therapeutic training is changing today, but certainly in the 1980s and 1990s, a lot of the training was problem-oriented or behavioral-oriented. The therapists who came out with us were fascinated by the ceremony and intrigued by how it might influence their own work.

The way of listening as a problem-oriented therapist is very different from the way we listen to people's stories after they come off the mountain. We listen for, "Who is this person? What's their way of walking in the world? What's their way of facing difficult times?" We listen for their gifts. We listen for what Spirit is telling them. It's seeing the beauty in a person's struggle, and being able to say, "Wow, you're going through changes, you're going through the underworld, and look what you're doing and how you are walking through this time! Keep going. You can do it." It's acknowledging and empowering the shadow and the struggle. It's all part of the wholeness.

I remember one training group we sent out in the afternoon to come back with stories and practice mirroring. One man told a beautiful story, full of peace, understanding, and comfort. The trainee who mirrored him was a very good therapist. His response was, "Where's the anger? There's no anger in this story. You're avoiding the anger."

The man who had told the story was crestfallen. We asked him, "How did that feel, to have your story mirrored that way?" He said, "I feel completely unseen. I feel like there's something wrong with me."

It was a great reminder and teaching to trust the story. If there was hidden anger, what he was given that day on his medicine walk was preparing him to see it. But in this case, this man, a man of peace who had done a lot of work in his life to get there, truly had no "anger issues" to deal with.

We've seen so many people go out in nature and be shown their real gifts. When that's mirrored back to them and affirmed, it gives them the strength to go even deeper. The process of having an important experience, telling the story in an environment where people are curious and listening, rather than judging and trying to fix them, is so empowering. It is such a rare way of listening in our modern lives.

Our friend, Derham, once said, "You know, the study of a caged animal is very different from studying an animal in its natural habitat. I feel that modern psychology is the study of the caged animal, and that's why it's so problem-oriented." He saw that the vision fast took people back into their natural habitat, and that spending three or four days alone brought out human wholeness in a way that we didn't often get in the civilized world. I always loved that.

We're raised to believe that, if your friend is sad, your role is to try to make that person happy again. You're supposed to fix the problem. So we feel burdened. I watch how young people quickly understand mirroring, and I see it's such a gift for them. Finally, they have a way of communicating with their peers that works, and removes the personal burden of needing to have "answers" or "be happy" so that their friend stays with them.

This makes me think that we're born with that kind of curiosity and listening. It's been bred out of us, and we have to relearn it. Steven and I have often said, "We're all 'mything' ourselves into being." This is what we humans do. We are always storying ourselves into being. And our story continues to change and to grow. Joseph Campbell wrote about it so well in *A Hero with a Thousand Faces*. We are the heroes of our own myth.

Steven talked about a moment when he was coming back from taking one of his first youth groups out to the desert. It had been a hard and deeply moving group, and Steven was feeling the awe of what had happened. He was driving home across the Golden Gate Bridge, and in the middle of the bridge, he suddenly had this overwhelming new awareness: "I am a vision fast guide!"

He was not really a vision fast guide. He barely knew what that meant. And yet, he felt the calling, and it became his story: I am a Vision fast guide. Over the years, he grew into it. It was somehow both a calling, and a part of what he yearned to grow into.

People on vision fast tend to have experiences of feeling called by who they yearn to be. Having that mirrored and given back to them empowers the person to live that yearning and to grow into it.

GUIDING AS A COUPLE

The love between Steven and me was strong and beautiful – and full of its ups and downs. For me, it was clear that a good relationship does not mean you don't have arguments or disagreements. Actually, that would be boring. Our relationship was never boring. There were really dark, painful times. There were really wonderful, beautiful times. And there were maybe three times in those 30 years when things got difficult enough that I thought, "Oh my God, this is shaking the very foundation of our relationship." Those few times when it did bring the foundation into question were important times. We had to renew and re-question if we were still meant to be together.

As we grew older, all this softened a bit. Neither of us was perfect. We had our wounds, we had our shadows, we made our mistakes, and we hurt each other. It was all part of it. Learning how to love is learning how to accept each other for being fallible. Steven was fallible. I was fallible. And yet, in the end, all I could say was that I just loved him. I just loved him. Love is not rational. I learned that to really love is accepting people for who they are.

One of the biggest gifts Steven gave to people was his humanness. He was not shy when it came to talking about his shadows. He loved people who embraced their shadows. It was about being human together. Many times I heard people say that Steven's generosity in showing his humanness made them better able to accept and love their own humanness.

Steven's life was not always an easy life. He lived a pretty painful life, all in all. Down deep at his core, there were a lot of self-worth questions. He had a lot of despair. He had such big ideals, and he never felt like he lived up to them. He never felt that he was quite good enough as a husband or father.

For a lot of us, when we feel not quite worthy enough, we might pretend that we're okay. But that wasn't Steven's way. Steven's way was to say, "Look at the horrible sides of me, too. Can you still love me anyway?" That was a pretty big gift.

At the same time, he was so generous – I think almost because of it. He had such a big heart, and when he loved people, he really loved them. How many times did he take people on as his son or daughter, because they grew up not having a good model? He said, "I'm going to be your father." He'd keep in touch with them, and he really cared. If someone showed up at the door, he was always there with them.

In a way, the love he shared was more real because it contained all the shadow. He knew what shadow was, and he was all too aware that he wasn't perfect enough. This made him, in my opinion, more capable of genuinely loving people in their humanness and expressing that love. He was not afraid to show his most vulnerable sides.

It's probably one of the things that impacted people the most, to feel like it was okay to be human. To have bumps, and wounds, and whatever it was. We could laugh together and hold each other and say, "Yeah, brother! We've done things we regret, and we have secrets. And we're still good people, and we can still love each other. We just keep trying." We took it on as a responsibility to be this way with people. We saw it as a gift of empowerment.

There was also that line that all guides have to deal with: when is sharing a few words about your own life or relationship going to serve the group, and when is it inappropriate? How do you keep it from interfering with being able to listen to the people? And how do you show up when you're feeling shitty? That's always a thin edge.

The other thread of doing this work as a couple was that, for certain people, maybe even more important than the solo, was that they saw a man and woman who were able to be real with each other, work together, support each other, and admit to having bumps in their relationship. Again and again, we were amazed at how much that modeling was what lingered for people. So many told us that they had rarely seen it in their own lives, which to us, was very sad.

As the years went by, there were more and more guides who chose to take out special populations, such as just working with women, or just working with men. Though we could see the value in this, it didn't feel like our calling. When we took out a mixed group, we always felt it was important that there be both a man and a woman to hold the container. Sometimes there were people in the group who had trust issues with one gender or another. It made them feel safer to have us both there.

Occasionally, Steven and I would come home from preparing a group to go out, and one of us would say, "Oh, my God, so-and-so never looked at me. She was always looking at you." Or, "Obviously, for so-and-so, nothing I say is ever the right thing." If a woman couldn't accept anything Steven said and was always looking to me, we saw that there was most likely something going on around her relationship with men. We didn't say, "Oh, we have to send her out there to look at that." It was just information we tucked away so that, when we listened to the story she brought back from her solo, we could be a better mirror for her.

We were seeing our culture go through real changes around relationships between men and women. There were new ideas about what a relationship looked like, new values around it, and new agreements.

Over the decades, we heard this evolution in people's stories. For many women coming through, the intent has been about claiming a woman's power and rejecting patriarchy. We also see men reclaiming their masculinity, and others who are questioning or affirming their gender identity or sexual orientation. It is exciting to see this evolution happening within the ceremony.

Often there were both men and women in the group who were going through the process of claiming their own worth and their own identity in new ways. When they witnessed each other's stories in a context that was empowering and non-judgmental, and where people could safely speak their truth, we saw a lot of healing.

How many times did we hear women say to the men in the group, "Oh my God, one of the biggest things I got during this time was hearing your stories and realizing, 'Wow! These are some really good men!'" And vice versa. Men often said, "I learned so much about women from hearing your stories."

For us, that felt really important. It was another article of clothing we could put on the bare bones of the ceremony. It engendered new experiences and understanding that people carried back into the world. We loved being part of that.

Part 4

Breathing

THE DOCUMENTARY

A number of people had asked if they could do a film about our work, including a film group from Japan. Our answer was always, "You've got to do the vision fast yourself first, and then we'll talk." And so everybody vanished into the woodwork, which was great, because we weren't all that interested in having a big production made of it.

Then in 1995, Kim Shelton, a woman we loved and deeply respected, who had fasted and done a number of trainings with us, asked if she could do a film. She is a skilled documentary filmmaker who had already done some beautiful films. To do something so personal is very delicate. But we trusted Kim.

This time, we said, "Yes. Let's explore it." We said "yes" because it was Kim, and we said "yes" because we saw that, if done well, it would be a wonderful outreach tool for our trainees to take back into their communities and schools.

The making of that documentary was probably one of the most difficult times in our relationship – in both the amount of work it required and the amount of stress that came with it. It coincided with the moment when Selene was about to leave home. Keenan was long gone, and Christian had left home a couple of years before to go to college.

Selene was our last child to leave, and that was huge emotionally. So on top of getting her ready, and getting ourselves ready to see her off for Bard College far away in upstate New York, we were setting up this documentary. We had a youth group, we had a training group that came a few days earlier and left a few days later, and we had the parents, who actually came out to base camp and were a part of the whole incorporation piece.

And then we had the film crew – wonderful Kim, along with Win Phelps, a guide at the School who had been a TV and film director, and who volunteered to help. Every day we had the camera and microphone in our faces. The camera and sound men were wonderful people, and they were sensitive to what was happening. They began to interact with the kids, becoming friends and mentors to them. But it was not an easy time.

Steven was amazing in helping to hold that documentary time together. He did really well. I think he, more than I, was good at being in front of the camera. He liked being in the spotlight. But it was exhausting. Absolutely exhausting. And it was frightening, because we were trying to hold this all together on every level. We were trying to do it as best we could, while at the same time, our daughter was leaving home.

When the last child leaves home it changes the relationship. It changes everything. This was one of those times – one of those very, very, very few times in all the 30 years we were together – that I had the feeling in the midst of the stress, "Oh my God, maybe the foundation isn't strong enough." We came home after a very long day with the group and stayed up late into the night trying to talk through it. We survived, and we became closer for it. But it was painful.

Out of that time came the beautiful gift of Kim's documentary. She did such a wonderful job, and she was so careful not to invade people's privacy for the three days and nights of the solo fast. The kids loved it! For them it was that feeling that somebody really wanted to hear them. They felt heard, and they felt seen, and they dropped into it in such a natural way. They were amazing, and they so well represented the youth who came through for this important life-marking ceremony.

Selene was one of the fasters in that group, which was another reason why it was all so woven together. It was a perfect time for her to mark leaving home, and it was a really important time for her. Within days of the end of the documentary and the last trainees leaving, Selene left. Steven drove her to the Las Vegas airport, and I literally fell to my knees and just sobbed. I was so cracked open from just having gone through three weeks of being really stretched. It all hit me when she went out the back door. My baby was leaving.

STEVEN'S ILLNESS

Steven began to notice that his breathing was becoming more difficult back in the early 1980s, shortly after we moved to Big Pine. It was frightening for him to not have the breath he used to have. Was this just part of aging? Was it because of his smoking? In retrospect, we would later see that this was the first indication of a serious illness.

As the internet became available in the 1990s, Steven began to do his own research on lung illnesses. He was the one who came up with the possibility that he might have Alpha-1 antitrypsin deficiency. He talked to our wonderful doctor in Bishop, who found out that there was a simple blood test Steven could take to see if this was a possibility. The blood test came back positive.

Back then, most doctors and very few people had ever heard of Alpha-1 Antitrypsin Deficiency. But someone who came from Colorado to train with us told us about an incredible hospital in Denver that specialized in respiratory illness. "You should come and stay with us and go to this hospital," he said.

So in 1998, we went to the National Jewish Health and Research Center in Denver. It was an amazing hospital, and a revelation to us. After two days of tests, including a genetic test, we were taken to an office and several doctors came in. They told us that they were pretty sure Steven had one of the more severe types of Alpha-1 Antitrypsin Deficiency, an inherited condition that eventually causes serious lung and liver disease. They were just waiting for the genetic test to be sure.

They were wonderful. As hard as it was to hear in some ways, we finally knew what it was, and that there were doctors who knew how to help. Steven was given new medication and some good solid suggestions for how to deal with it, including the use of oxygen. Later, the genetic tests came back to confirm their diagnosis. There was no cure for Steven's illness.

Around this time, we were blessed to find a very unique and beautiful piece of property for sale south of Big Pine. Since our dear friend, Gigi Coyle, was also looking for "home," we sent a fax to her where she was on her sailboat in Mexico. Steven wrote one of his irresistible, golden-tongued letters insisting that, "This is the place!" and telling her to come immediately.

So she came, and we all went to see it for the first time. As we were walking the property, we stopped to sit on a bench at the far side of the little lake, looking across at the house. Steven suddenly said, "This is a place where I could die." Gigi and I looked at each other, nodding, "Done," we both thought.

It had become a real challenge for Steven to have people coming to the house all the time, and he needed quiet and privacy, so it was a blessing to spend those years at the place now known as "Three Creeks." To be able to have that beautiful place, and to share it with Gigi, was such a gift. I kept busy with gardening, clearing deadfall, keeping the creek clear and running. It was non-stop, taking care of five acres of land, but it made me happy to get my hands dirty, raking leaves and fixing things around the property.

From then on, we began to step back from the amount of trainings we were doing, giving ourselves more time to focus on creating a lifestyle that best supported Steven, and my own needs to be there with him. We lived there for about four years, and we had time to just be with each other. Year by year, Steven's breathing was getting more and more difficult, and he was having to let go of more identities. There were a lot of changes in his life, and it was a very difficult journey for him.

WIDENING THE CIRCLE

Another thread of our work was creating support systems for guides. Ron Pevny, who had trained with us at Rites of Passage, Inc. and was beginning to do the work on his own, wrote to us and said, "You know, there are so many people doing this work now throughout the United States, we should get together. Will you help do this?"

"Yes," we said. So we all contacted the guides we knew, and we had our first meeting of the Wilderness Guides Council in 1987, when Selene was ten. We met in the Saline Valley in the winter of that year – sitting in the hot springs. That began what has become the annual Wilderness Guides Gathering. The intent was to share how we were each doing this work, and to get inspired by each other, avoiding that human trait of feeling competitive.

We spoke to that trait of competition, asking, "How can we support each other?" which inevitably would help to fill everyone's groups. "The more we cooperate," we said, "the more people we're going to reach."

The second intent, which worked for a little while and then faded out, was about sensitivity for overuse of the land. We asked, "How can we share where we're going to bring our groups, and what base camp we're going to use, in a way that people won't use our places, and to ensure that a certain area won't be overused?" We had many conversations about how to become guardians of the land we used.

Our international work began with Gigi Coyle bringing groups from Germany. The Germans seemed especially intrigued about losing their borders. With the first European groups coming to the Valley, the word began to get back to Europe about what we were doing, and every year for a while we had a group from there.

The word got further out, and then people began to come to train and take it back to Germany, Switzerland, Austria, South Africa, and England, mostly taking advantage of the more comprehensive, immersive month-long training. With that sort of international flavor, we deepened our exploration of how to bring differing cultural roots into this ceremony in a meaningful way. That was a fun exploration to do with the Europeans coming through, and it was always exciting to see the amazing people who were attracted to bringing this work back to their own organizations. They came with so many skills and gifts.

When people began to ask us to come to Europe to teach, for a long time, we said, "No. Our work is here, on this land of our base camps. People have to come to us."

And then Selene went through her dark phase as she entered the teenage years, and she didn't communicate much. She was really trying to find her own unique identity.

One of the things she really wanted to do was go to London. So we decided it was a good time in her life to travel – not only to take her to England where some of our trainees were living, but to cultures where even the language was different. It felt so ripe a time for Selene to experience being in another culture, and to have a sense of the bigger world beyond our little desert town. So we accepted some teaching offers in both England and Germany.

A few years later, in 1999, we were invited to South Africa by our dear friends and former trainees, Judy Bekker and Valerie Morris. They invited us to do a youth training through Educo Africa, a youth development organization that helped young people, especially those at risk, to discover and live their potential. We couldn't resist. It was such an important opportunity to meet the amazing South Africans who had lived through the institutionalized racial segregation and discrimination of apartheid, which had only recently ended.

Amazing people. It just touched us so deeply. It was exciting to feel that we could support these people who were doing so much for their communities, especially with the enormous impact of AIDS in their villages.

After we returned home, we raised money from our School's community to bring one of the men from that group, Coleridge Samuel Daniels, who had done so much for the kids on Cape Town's streets, back to Big Pine to do the month-long training at the School. When he returned to South Africa, Educo Africa hired him to bring more of the rites-of-passage orientation to their organization. Others from Educo Africa came to the month-long training in the years following that.

Even as Steven was getting more and more challenged by his

health, as hard as it was and as tiring as it was, doing seminars outside of the country somehow wasn't as tiring to him as doing trainings and all of our administrative work running the School at home. All we had to do was to show up, and our former trainees, who had asked us to come, did all the organizing and registration.

They really took such good care of Steven. They carried his oxygen machine, helped him up and down the stairs, and were supportive all the way. He always had someone right there to help him out, which certainly supported me, as well. He could sit for a two-hour meeting with a group, and then go back to our room and sleep for five hours. We didn't have the additional weight of running an organization, and he really enjoyed the international people, who also adored him.

We were teaching in Europe when Steven started a conversation with Haiko Nitschke about creating something similar to our Wilderness Guides' Council internationally. Haiko had trained at the School in the early 1990s and had become a very successful vision fast guide and trainer in Europe. He founded the ÖKOSYS Institute for Ecological System Education. He was also the translator for a number of Steven's books into German, and a good friend for many years.

Steven and Haiko talked deep into the night about what a rich conversation it would be to bring together guides from many countries, including other cultures. Now that there were people from many places in the world, and in many different cultures, who offered a modern version of the vision fast, it felt like good timing.

We tried to set it up ourselves, but it became clear that Steven was just too sick, and we wouldn't be able to do it. We were lamenting this to a month-long training group made up of all Europeans that had come to Death Valley in the early spring of 2002. They said, "We'll do it."

That group of trainees went back and made the first International Guides Network Gathering happen in the fall of that year, just a few months before Steven died. Amazing. Even though Steven was on oxygen 24 hours a day and very sick, he wanted to be there. I said, "Steven, we don't have to do this. I told the sponsors that if you're just too sick when the time comes to leave, we have to say no."

But he was sure. "I want to do it," he said. From the space he was in at that time, which was often full of despair, where he could hardly walk or think, he pulled together the energy to help me make it happen. And our dear friends who were the sponsors made sure everything was ready when we arrived.

Being able to see and feel what he had been a major part of making possible was so big for him. And the beautiful way they honored Steven as Elder and teacher brought him – and me – to tears. But I really broke down when they came together to sing him the beautiful German song, "Ferryman," and they ceremonially gave him a pfennig to pay the Ferryman to get him across the river. It just broke me.

There was a part of Steven that feared people would forget him, that he hadn't really made an impact. I think the international gathering was one of those moments at the end of his life when he really got that his work had made an impression, and that it was going to keep going. That was so important for him.

One of the last things he tried to do was to create an international web in which all the countries could stay in communication with each other. He had this master vision of global support and inspiration that would be more than just one gathering every two years. There were some wonderful meetings and talks about it, but it was so big that it didn't happen before he died.

In those last years, we began to think a lot more about how to bring rites-of-passage work and end-of-life work together. How do we support people who are dying? How does the rites-of-passage ceremony support people at the end of their life? Where does preparation overlap for the end of physical life, and for the significant symbolic deaths during our lives?

Steven wrote some wonderful outlines on how to go into rest homes, nursing homes, and places where people were dying, and create ceremonies – how to wheelchair them outside under a tree for an hour, and give them these ways of preparing to die, to support them, and to support their families. We talked a lot about that, because it was what we were living with.

The last group we did together was in Death Valley, with a group of hospice doctors, nurses, volunteers, and chaplains. We did the four-night vision fast, but with the overlay of what Storm had given Ginnie, as a way of preparing to die: Decision Road, Death Lodge, Purpose Circle, In-between. We encouraged them, as they went through this process, to drop as best they could into feeling as if they really were going to die, so they could have more understanding and empathy with the people they worked with.

The dream was always that Steven and I would have the time to develop this more. He was, to the end, full of ideas and visions about how to keep making this work happen in the world. He was such a visionary.

ONE MORE POEM

Those 20 years in the valley were a prolific time for Steven's writing. At his core, he most deeply identified himself as Writer and Poet. In the last days of his life, when asked what kept him going, he said that besides loving his family one day longer, there might be one more poem.

Steven wrote *The Roaring of the Sacred River* when we moved to Big Pine, as our "training manual." It was picked up by Harper & Row, who also had *The Book of the Vision Quest* by that time. They are still the publisher for *The Book of the Vision Quest* after all these years. It's been in print since 1980. They dropped *The Roaring of the Sacred River* after about a year, so we bought it back and have it available through Lost Borders Press. Later, Steven wrote *The Four Shields,* a really important book that took a number of years to write. In it we refined a lot of our training methods. And always, the books catalyzed a lot of new learning for us. Always.

As Steven's breathing became more difficult and he was feeling the quickening of his death, he finally wrote a book that, for me, was the first book where he really let his soul shine: *We Who Have Gone Before – Memory and an Old Wilderness Midwife.* Memory was an aspect of God to Steven. He wondered if perhaps the immortality of soul was in the memories that were left behind in each of us and literally in the land. It's such a beautifully poetic, personal book. He gave himself permission to do this, rather than write another book that would help the work, and this was really great.

His very last book was called *Bound for the Crags of Ithaka.* As the *Odyssey* was a very important book for him, one of his dreams as a young man was to write an epic poem about the *Odyssey* and what it meant to him. It wasn't easy writing that book, because when one doesn't have enough oxygen, the mind doesn't work so well. It became more of a struggle for him, but he kept at it, even when the formerly fluent typist could only type with one finger at a time.

The *Ithaka* book was both the fulfillment of a dream and the wish that it might help financially support me after his death. The price of that book is much too high, the wing and a prayer that I would be ok when he was gone. When he died, *Ithaka* was at the printers. Our wonderful book designer, Sarah Underhill, made it happen that the first box of that last book was delivered in time for his memorial. Such a gift.

TRANSFORMING THE SCHOOL

There came a point in the 1990s when we decided that, in order to focus more on the training, it was time to bring in some people we really trusted to take out the open vision fasts.

We called in Emerald North, Silvia Talavera, and Joseph Lazenka, who had all trained at the School. Joseph had been working for the Bear Tribe for years. Em had a lifetime of experience in ceremony, and Silvia was gifted. We trusted that these three were perfectly capable of signing up their own people and taking full responsibility for the logistics and running of each group. We would provide the insurance, permits, mailing list, bookkeeping, etc.

While this arrangement grew the School and enabled us to focus more on the training program, it also added more administrative work. Our dear friend, Gigi, was also important during that time. We were always trying to find new names to call Gigi in order to keep her a part of the School, because she was just so invaluable. She was our ally. Sometimes we called her our Associate Director, and sometimes she was a fellow guide and trainer.

As the School grew, Emerald, Silvia, Gigi, and Joseph took on some of the established training programs, as well. But Steven was getting sicker, so it was harder for him to do his usual part of the administrative work.

Inevitably, I was doing most of everything. I had a frightening moment at base camp when I was waiting at the threshold circle waiting for people to return from their solo. I felt no excitement at all. Only tiredness. I felt so deeply that this wasn't fair to the people. It had all gotten to be too much. We realized, for the third significant time, if it's "not working for the family," then we have to change the work.

The central focus of our family had become Steven's progressive illness and his dying. In order to give that the room it needed, we had to change something. There was a moment when we looked at each other while talking about how hard it was getting, and we both knew at the same time: "We have to give the School away." We just knew it. Thank God for those moments of shared knowing.

Sometime in 2001, we wrote out, as fully as we could, all the things the administrator of the School needs to do: Steven's tasks, my tasks, and everything that would be necessary to turn it over to someone else. We had our annual scheduling meeting in our home with most of our staff, including Gigi, Emerald, Silvia, Joseph and Win. We surprised them by starting the meeting with handing them this list we had put together. We said that we just could no longer run the School with Steven's health and with the growth of the School. Similar to what we had done at Rites of Passage, Inc., we said, "If you want the School, in whatever form you want to create it, it's yours." We let them know that we included Mary McHenry, Jeffrey Duvall, Jack West, and John Davis to participate if they felt called.

"And if none of you wants it," we said, "we will need to cut the School back to just the trainings that Steven and I can still do, so it's not as much administrative work. We just can't do it anymore."

We let them know that we would continue to run the School for one more year as they figured out what they wanted to do and had the time to put things together to take over.

Over the next year, Emerald, Joseph, Silvia, Win, and Gigi continued to meet to create a new form for the School. We didn't attend any of these meetings, feeling that if you give something away, you give it away with no conditions. It was completely up to them. Of course, Steven couldn't resist writing up "Some thoughts on how to continue to ensure the School's success, by Steven."

During that year, we continued to run the School, transferring information when they asked and giving them more of the administrative work when we were teaching in Europe. And then, at the end of the year, we backed out. By then, they had decided on the new form of the School: Joseph and Emerald were Co-Directors, with the others guiding and supporting as best they could.

Our agreement was that Steven and I would do the trainings we wanted to do and keep the money we made. By this time, the only work that really excited Steven was teaching in Europe, the month-long training, and working with people dealing with life-threatening illnesses and those tending to people at the end of life.

WHEN IS IT ENOUGH?

We understood that Steven's illness was progressive, and that nothing could make him better. I saw through Steven that suffocation is one of the most frightening experiences there is. With every breath, he became aware that he was dying. And it was only getting worse.

We knew that what we were doing was preparing for his death, which meant living as fully as we could while he was here. But underneath that was the constant awareness that he was dying.

A lot of our understandings around rites-of-passage work, including Ginnie's preparing to die and other experiences around death, informed the way we walked through this – such as having the courage to know when it was time to give the School away.

We had to really stay focused on the most important things with Steven. We recognized that some of his biggest work was grieving and mourning the loss of identity, after identity, after identity. He faced questions like, "Who am I now? Am I important at all? Is there any meaning left in my life?"

That process so clearly strengthened the work we did with other people. There's a certain poignancy about being that close to death, walking that edge. Steven was so amazing as he shared his journey of being conscious to his dying. The conversations around death were in everything we did.

The big question for him was, "When is it enough?" The whole question around chosen death inevitably came up – both because of what we had witnessed with Ginnie, and because the times were changing. There was more talk about physician-assisted suicide, and Steven was really looking at that, almost every day. He knew that if he said, "It's enough," I would support him, and that we would find a way to make that happen. I saw how that enabled him to keep choosing every day.

"How much is too much?" I heard him say. "When it gets to be that I need oxygen 24 hours a day, that's enough." And then I watched him hit that point, look around, and take another step. "When I can't clean myself, and I can't get out of bed, then it's enough." And he got pretty close to that. I had the sense of how we can never know what's too much – or what's needed – until we get there.

Steven was walking this way with every breath, feeling his death upon him – and the terror of that, and the loss. He was a man who had not chosen a life about learning how to become unattached. His life was about being fiercely attached. That was a chosen way. When he had an emotion, it was a big emotion, and when he was down, and dark, and scared, it was big. When he loved, with his huge, generous heart, he really loved. Learning how to let go of those things that he fiercely loved – including me and Selene and our family – was really painful and difficult.

In the last year and a half, he needed constant oxygen, had medications that helped a little, had more and more difficulty walking even a few steps, and his mind wasn't working right because it was oxygen-deprived. The conversations of our life were about death. We went to teach in Europe, and it didn't matter what the theme of the seminar was, it was clear that people came because they knew it might be their last time with Steven.

I tried to keep our track loosely on the theme of the seminar, and there was Steven sitting next to me, talking about his dying. And it was great! It didn't matter if it was relevant or not. It was wise, and he wasn't turning away. He might have been afraid. But he didn't turn away. He didn't hide it. He showed it. There was a beautiful teaching in it for the people who were around him.

In 2001, Steven took a solo Death Lodge month, oxygen tank in tow. He was hoping to show himself and me that he could still take care of himself. And he wanted to "make it good" with his relationships as a preparation for his death.

One of the people he wanted to see was Hyemeyohsts Storm. He wanted to see Storm and say, "Thank you, and if I hurt you in any way, I'm sorry." We finally found him, and he agreed to meet. Steven told him how much he appreciated him, and he thanked him for being what he was in our life. Storm expressed a lot of respect for Steven. It was an important completion for Steven, and for us.

He also visited others who were important in his life, such as his children, siblings, previous wives, and friends. When he returned home, he was seriously sick, and he said that he hadn't meant to do his

Death Lodge quite so literally. He finally had to admit that he needed me, and a support system, to help care for him.

Grandpa Raymond was also sick during Steven's last years, and Steven called and asked him to come over. They sat together, and Steven apologized for any way that he might have hurt Grandpa Raymond. And Grandpa Raymond apologized for any way that he might have hurt Steven and me. It was beautiful to watch this easy ability to express love and acceptance of each other. There wasn't anything specific that either of them had done that needed to be apologized for, but it was making it good and expressing the respect they had for each other.

In the last years of his life, Steven had to face his biggest monsters: self-doubt, feelings of inadequacy, jealousy, and guilt. It seemed they reared up bigger than ever in those last years. And in the last months of his life, he seemed to finally make peace with himself. I saw that there is such a thing as "healing into death" when there is a certain consciousness about dying. Another gift from Steven.

SEA LEVEL

After that last trip to Death Valley in the winter of 2002, our doctor said, "Steven, if you want to live longer, you need to go to sea level."

"Okay," I said. "Let's pack up a few things, let's call a few people, and let's move back to the Bay Area."

Steven's best friend had an empty house up above Santa Rosa, so that's where we first went. It was interesting – and a little sad for me – to see that for Steven, this was his confirmation that I really loved him. For our whole life together, he was scared that I didn't really love him, and I would leave him. He *knew* I loved him, but he didn't fully believe it underneath. For me, it was obvious that wherever we go, we go together. I was so glad that it also had him finally realize that we were together to the end, and that I loved him through the hard times, as well as the times of magic we created together.

So we moved to that house up above Santa Rosa, but the elevation was still too high, and it was isolated. If there had been an emergency, it would have taken too long to get up or down that windy road. So we moved into his friend's personal home, and his friend moved into a trailer. We lived there for a while, but we felt uncomfortable taking his home. And there were too many people coming through the house, which was difficult for Steven. So I asked him, "Okay, where can you imagine being that you'd really be comfortable?"

He told me that he would be comfortable at my parents' home, not far away in Mill Valley. They had a little apartment underneath the porch of their house, where my two sisters and I had our room when we were growing up. It had big glass doors and windows that looked out on a tiny deck and huge redwood trees. It was quiet, and it was private. So that's where we went.

That apartment was so tiny, we didn't have room to do much of anything but be together. We brought in a little hot plate to cook our food, and for a while, Steven could breathe a little easier. My parents were so gracious. They pretty much left us to our own devices, and Steven felt much more comfortable.

A few months later, it all happened so quickly. He got a cold, the antibiotics didn't seem to be helping, and thank God, we had already done a lot of talking about what he wanted and what he didn't want. He had very clearly said, "I never want to go to the hospital again." So when it got to the point where he really couldn't talk anymore, at least I knew what he wanted.

We brought in a second oxygen machine, and we did everything as best we could to make him comfortable. In the end, he so consciously said goodbye. But in these last two days, I was in denial. I thought he'd get well again.

The night before his last day was a terrible, terrible night. He just couldn't breathe. He fought for each breath. He tried to get up, to get *out*. Finally he stretched his arms out wide and surrendered, falling back on the bed, even though lying down was one of the most difficult positions for him to breathe. He immediately fell asleep, and I laid down next to him and just listened for his breath. When dawn finally came, he woke up and motioned for me to help him get up. He held on to my shoulder and I to him. He wanted me to open the sliding glass doors.

We walked onto the little balcony and he just looked out. That was the moment when I knew he knew. This was it. He was saying goodbye to the land.

I brought him back in from outside and then, to our surprise, Selene walked in the door with a big smile on her face. He turned and he looked at her. This look of utter joy and disbelief came over his face, and his very last word was, "Selene."

It was his goodbye to Selene. She came over and took him and held him. He put his arm around her shoulder and I walked back around the table.

And then he looked at me. He looked at me, and I'll never forget this. I'd never seen anything like it before. His look was saying, "This is it. THIS IS IT!" with utter love, and utter recognition.

Then he sat down on the bed near the table, leaning on the table, with his arms holding him up. From then on, he didn't talk. He was ready to fight. But he wasn't fighting to live. He was fighting to die. He pulled at each breath, head down. And it was hard work, such hard work. He was fierce. He fought hard. It wasn't going gently into that good night. It was fighting for every breath. He fought all day.

Scott Eberle, MD, our hospice doctor who had become a friend, was there in the last five hours to guide us through. He made sure the final battle was as brief, easy, and painless as possible. And some of the other people who he loved began to appear: my brother Jay, my mother, Gigi, his dear friend, Howard. We cleared the table of all his medications, we read poetry out loud, we sat next to him and said goodbye. It was a beautiful room full of people who were there, for unknown and perfect reasons, to hold him. Close family.

This last fight was so like Steven. It was big, it was conscious, and it was done with all of who he was. It was not half-way. It was dusk when he took his final, and quiet, last breath. Someone lit a candle and put it out on the balcony.

It was May 6, 2003. Steven had lived to age 64.

Part 5

Death is Sacred
in All its Forms

MEREDITH

When Steven died, everything died. I died. It was really clear. I felt like I had no footprint anymore. All the footprints behind me had blown away, and I had no orientation anymore.

For the first week or two, I was so broken open – all emotions so big and so painful. I was so full of love. I was so full of pain. I was so full of not knowing.

I remember that on one of those first days, some of us walked downtown. We were going to go look for an urn for Steven's ashes. The others went into a store, and I was leaning against something at the edge of the sidewalk. A young man walked past me. I was just watching what was going on, and he went a little bit beyond me, then he turned around and he looked at me and said, "You know, I have never, ever, in my entire life, felt anyone who's looked at me with so much love." And then he turned around and he walked on. I realized that I was so open, so cracked open, that the love and the pain were all the same. They were all huge.

The first week was about calling the family, who dropped everything to be with us. Steven would have been amazed and deeply touched to have been sent off by them. We had two different memorials that week. One of them was at the crematorium, where they let us open the casket, put offerings in with him, and say whatever words needed to be said. They let us roll him into the oven, and I was able to flip the final switch. That was so important, as one of Steven's biggest fears was being burned. It felt right that I could be the one to flip the switch.

As we stood outside and watched the smoke rise from the chimney, I thought of how, for Steven, Spirit is breath. And here it was, released to the skies over the lush green mountains of Mt. Tamalpais. I can't easily put to words how I was feeling. Certainly I didn't realize I had such an infinite, bottomless well of tears, grief, love, gratitude, pain. Certainly I had never realized how important having family to support me and each other could be.

For me, that first week was all about how to be there for the family. I couldn't sleep at night. I just kept showing up for what I had to do. Selene slept with me, we held hands, and she was so sweet. I remember one of those mornings, I had hardly slept and we had the family again that day, which was great, but Selene looked at me and I said, "Selene, I don't know if I can carry all this." She came over and she literally lifted me up, off the floor. It helped. It was so beautiful.

I don't know how I would have gotten through that time if I hadn't had the context of recognizing that I was in the midst of one of the biggest rites of passage of my life. To feel as if I had died was appropriate, because my life as it had been had completely ceased to exist. I had been with Steven since my early twenties. We shared everything: family, work, friendship, sickness – just everything. I knew it wasn't wrong to feel that, but I was amazed at the strength of it. I felt almost like there was this magnetic pull into the black hole he'd vanished into, that I didn't understand. I didn't want to die. Not really. And yet, that magnetic pull was incredible.

For a month or so it all felt surreal. I could look out the window and feel like I could go between being in the world where Steven was still there, and being in this world where he was gone. I can't describe it, except that it was absolutely surreal. It wasn't just the mind. It was an entire body experience of two worlds, and of being caught between them.

I couldn't make any decisions. I didn't know what I wanted, I didn't know who I was, I didn't know anything. Fortunately – and I was aware of this – I didn't have little kids to take care of. I felt for mothers or fathers who have to deal with young children at the same time. I had no responsibilities except for very basic ones, and to my daughter, who was a grown woman.

I also didn't have responsibilities to the School, because we had already given it away. My last commitment had been to a month-long training group I'd planned to do with Steven. We'd finally said, "Hey, it might not happen." And it didn't happen, because Steven died a couple of days before we were supposed to start.

For quite a few months I couldn't read anything, I couldn't watch movies or television, I couldn't listen to anything except music. It was a crazy experience. On the outside, I probably looked pretty steady, though prone to breaking out into sobs. I was full of so many emotions that were processing through me that there was no room for anything else. All I could do was keep trying to show up every day for whatever emotion was there that day. And trust that if I just kept showing up for it, it was moving me towards the new world.

There was the ongoing experience of disorientation. I walked a lot. It was the only way I could process all the emotion going through me, but I got lost over and over in places that I knew perfectly well. Again, it was such a mirror for me being lost inside. My short-term memory was completely gone. Frighteningly so. There was no room in me for it. There was only room for these huge emotions, wave after wave after wave. I kept showing up for them, feeling them, being with them, and not pushing them away. That's all I could do.

Through the next years there was a part of me that was witnessing what I was going through in a kind of curious awe. That helped me, too. I had developed that sense of a non-judgmental witness through the many years I'd been doing this work, and now that became an ally for me. It was that part of me that watched and said, "Wow! Look at what's happening!"

WHO AM I NOW?

I can say, in retrospect, that what I was doing for those first several years was growing up all over again, into the new world. For those first months, I was like a child. My self-confidence was on the floor. There was a hunger to be touched, so that I felt I existed somehow. I could only depend on my emotions to inform me, as my mind and psyche were constantly changing and unreliable.

The South Shield. I'm not the kind of person who asks for help much, but now I felt needy inside. I was a child looking around and asking, "What is this? Where am I safe? What does this new world look like? What do I want? What's mine anymore?"

Almost every night I was sobbing, with so much pain. I had to become friends with pain in a way that I had never had to make friends with pain before. It took me a few years, but I came to finally feel pain as my friend that helped me feel alive and process what was flooding through me. We made a kind of gentle peace.

Then there were months of, "Who am I now? What am I supposed to do? Where are the 'yes's' that don't make me feel ill? And what are my values? How have they changed? What is important?"

The West Shield. Questions. Questions. Questions. I got so sick of it, over and over again. Until finally, one night I was so sick of it, I just cried and sobbed and yelled, I was so angry. I finally fell asleep curled up in a fetal position. The next morning I woke up, and there were no more questions. All that was left was, "How do I create a lifestyle that supports me now?"

The North Shield. For the next months it was all about, "What do I need? How do I create an environment that supports who I am now?" It wasn't that I decided to do this. It's just where I was.

Beginning the year Steven died, I returned to the practice of annually going out on fast, something we'd had to stop doing several years earlier because it had become too hard for Steven. This really helped me process the huge changes that were going on inside of me.

And then, probably four years after Steven died, I couldn't figure out why, after all I'd done, I felt like there was still this deep, deep despair at the very core of me. My life was pretty good, my work felt good, and I no longer lived in the constant world of pain. I didn't understand why there was still this big blanket of despair.

That year, I went out on solo to ask about it. The first day of my fast was just despair. Nothing felt meaningful. Everything felt flat. I felt alone and empty. The next morning, I woke up early and from my sleeping bag, I looked around. I felt again the sense of everything being just flat and dead. There was a begging inside of me for help, for understanding.

Suddenly, out of seemingly nowhere, everything took on color: the pinions and junipers, the rocks, the ground – and something came into me. I don't want to put too many words to it, but suddenly the world became three-dimensional. It was that last piece to fall into place as I grew up into this new world.

The East Shield. Feeling connected with what is "bigger," with mystery, with all things. It was the last piece, and finally I didn't feel alone. I felt connected. There was such a huge relief. It wasn't dramatic at all, it was simple, simply was. For those next three days of solo, there was just simple peace in me, and a sense that the world was alive, each and every piece, and I had a relationship with it all. Belonging.

This was a great teaching for me, of literally watching myself go around the wheel and grow into the new world. It wasn't a decision of, "Okay, now it's time for the West!" It was only in retrospect that I could see that this was how my nature was processing something so huge.

This is how it works. Such a big teaching. If I just keep showing up, it moves me. Nature – and my nature – moving toward balance and healing. We had been teaching this for years, but I learned more about what a rite of passage really is during those years than I ever had in all the years we had been taking groups out. I lived it in some very essential way.

BEING HUMAN

Death was an important theme woven throughout Steven's and my life. This was a time in our culture when the taboo of talking about and acknowledging death, both physical and symbolic, was slowly being broken. This came after several generations had experienced so much death in the wars that many just had to shut down, both in talking about death and in processing the overwhelming grief.

Slowly, through the hospice movement, more people chose to die at home. With that came a lot of fear, and a lack of role-modeling for the ability to deal with the ego death involved in grieving, loss, and pain. There was a sense of, "If I go inside to feel the pain, the grief, and the mourning that is so overwhelming, I won't be able to handle it."

It's interesting that, at the same time Elisabeth Kübler-Ross came out with her five stages of grief and the hospice movement began, there was also a return to the old ways of marking ego death and symbolic death – rites-of-passage work.

You read in a lot of different indigenous writing that the rite-of-passage ceremony is a dying practice. Marking these significant transitions of our life and doing the hard work of dying to what was, of stepping into the scary place of the unknown in order to be born into the new, is seen as an important way of getting ready for the big transition: physical death.

Death has been so often used as a part of important rite-of-passage ceremonies. The most important thing a guide, or an initiator, can do in preparing somebody for an initiation, is to get them to the point where they feel as if they could die. And yet, they don't.

Death is a catalyst. It's the Great Transformer. The closer you can push up against it, the more possibility of transformation there is. So the more that we, as guides, can push the initiates to a place where their fear is big (yet their intention is bigger), and they feel as if they might die during threshold time, the more transformative the experience can be.

When I met Steven, it was very clear from the beginning that he was fascinated by death. There were a number of times he thought seriously about suicide before I met him. Part of that was because he was an emotional man who had a lot of shadow in him. But it soon became clear to me that it was also because he was fascinated by death.

As we fell in love, one of the things we often talked about was, "There's going to come a time when one of us goes first." Having to say goodbye was a realization. If we really love, if we allow ourselves to really love, one day one of us is going to say goodbye to the other. I can't think how many times that came into our conversations and awareness. That sense of foreboding was with us, even from the very beginning. Part of it, of course, was when you love deeply, you fear the pain of the loss of that person. That was reinforced by watching Aldie and Ginnie die.

I've been intimately involved in the dying and death of nine people close to me. In each death, there's always a teaching that comes with it about grieving. Each person does it differently. There's something so important about learning how to grieve, and to really process loss and pain, rather than being terrified by it and trying to avoid it. To grieve the loss of someone whom I loved very much, so many times in my life, has taught me a lot about being human.

ALDIE

In retrospect, there were so many important pieces about the experience of my father's death, one being that Steven and I got to share at least the last several days of it. This was a significant event, obviously, in my life, and it became one in Steven's life, too. Part of it was seeing the love between Ginnie and Aldie, and then watching one of them have to lose the other. The other part was to have the dying and death happen at home, rather than in a hospital. It was a very intimate and personal experience. The example that Ginnie set for how you can hold somebody at home and support people when they're dying taught me how to do that.

I was also able to see, in my father's last days, his "death lodge" and "purpose circle" work, and to see how naturally one does this as a way of surrendering to death. When an old friend came into his room to say goodbye, Aldie often said something so simple and essential about their friendship, and then drifted off somewhere else.

When he suddenly returned, pointing and motioning and mumbling, I asked, "Aldie, what are you doing? What's going on?" He often said there was a battle going on between love and death, or that he was making peace with himself.

The night before he died, he began to mumble, "Okay, I'm ready." There was a sense in him of self-acceptance. Of self-integration. Aldie was a man who carried a lot of guilt, and in his dying, there was a healing into death. With Aldie, I first saw that death lodge activity of making it good with oneself.

So later, when Storm gave us that Native American formula when we asked about Ginnie's preparation to die, it resonated with us immediately, because we'd seen it. We could say, "Oh, that's what was happening with Aldie." It was the same ingredients that enable people to die a symbolic death. The same processes of surrendering to physical death are naturally the same needed for surrendering to other life transitions. Again, it was all woven together.

I really got, after a number of personal deaths in my life, that each death left behind a kind of gift. I think that when my father died, the gift he left me was the courage to love, despite the potential loss.

It is so true, that right next to death is love. It felt like my commitment to Steven and losing my father were almost like one thing. It felt like I was given the gift of the love of my life at the same moment as my father's death.

GINNIE

Aldie and Ginnie's love for each other built rich soil for my relationship with Steven. They both took responsibility for living their love and their deepest dreams, and in dying a conscious death.

Ginnie grieved deeply after Aldie died. When I lost Steven, I understood what she went through. And yet, though she'd promised to follow him in death, she knew to wait until the grieving was done in order to check this story out. She didn't want to die out of grief. She didn't want to die out of hopelessness. She wanted to die as an affirmation, as a sense of fulfillment. There was a great teaching in that.

Chosen death. What is a chosen death? I still work with that today. That sense of knowing that it is time to die to something in your life, and having the courage to do the hard work of dying to it, even when you don't know what's going to come. There was that teaching in Ginnie's death. She knew that, for her, it was time to die. She believed that she would be joining Aldie, yet she didn't *really* know. It was an unknown.

We watched her consciously prepare her loved ones and try to make it good with the people she cared about in her life. Some of them were very angry with her for choosing to die, and she sat with them. She didn't try to make them not angry with her. She stood behind what she knew, and she expressed her love by just being there with them.

For Ginnie, joy was associated with death. There was excitement in the rebirth for her. That was a big teaching. She stepped joyfully into her death, even though she didn't know what was going to happen. She taught us about having courage to step into the unknown.

The gift she left for Steven and me at the door of her death was first, the knowing that it was time to leave Novato. Second, it was the specific knowing that our next move would be to Big Pine. Ginnie's death gave us the courage to say, "The time is now. Let's not wait until we think we've done everything perfectly. Now is the time."

EVELYN

The next significant death was Evelyn Eaton. She was trained by Grandpa Raymond's father at the same time that Raymond was. She and Raymond were close friends. She did nature-based wisdom work and ceremony, and she was seen as the Grandmother of this movement in the 1970s and 1980s. She was an amazing writer, and she wrote some beautiful books.

We met Evelyn at a Sun Bear gathering in the San Francisco Bay Area. She had moved to Independence, just south of Big Pine, shortly before we moved to the Valley. She invited us to come and do a ceremony with her up in the hills to bring healing to the earth, and we became close with her. A few times we stopped by her home with our fasting group before driving all the way back to Marin County, and she did a sweat for us.

Soon after we moved to Big Pine, she became sick, and very quickly it was clear that she was dying. Just as she was a teacher in so many ways in her life, she also was a great teacher in her death.

One thing I marvel at is that all of the deaths that were significant for us were home deaths. Not all that common in those days. Evelyn Eaton was one of those examples. She was dying, and so she called her women. There was a gathering of women around her that came and lived with her for support during her last months. They were there to do everything for her, which was very beautiful to watch. Her daughter was also there, helping her mother.

At one point, Evelyn called in a woman who was a nurse. She was the first person we met who called herself a "dying midwife." We'd never heard that term before, but we'd already begun to refer to the role that we did in our guiding as "midwifing." It was clear that guiding is a midwifery skill, but we'd never heard the term "dying midwife" before.

After Evelyn died, this woman came to visit us and we asked her about it. She told us that she helped Evelyn get psychologically ready to let go. She sat with her and had her talk about anything she still felt unresolved about, and helped her get current with her life so that she could finally slip away. She also had the medical skills to make it physically easier, and the ability to see the bigger picture without being quite so personally involved. So she could provide support in whatever made Evelyn more comfortable.

We asked her, "How did you become a dying midwife?" She smiled. "Most people don't know that's what I am," she said. "I'm really a nurse, but there was a time, a number of years ago, when I was very, very depressed."

She told us that one day, she went home to her apartment, drank a whole bottle of liquor, and took a whole bottle of pills – plenty enough to kill her – and had gone unconscious and died. She had the experience of a big light and being pulled into the tunnel. And then there was a point when a message came to her. She was told, with no judgment at all, "Hey! You can come. It's a beautiful place here in this light. Or let me show you what was missing in your life." And she saw, like a film, all the times she had not hugged someone. Picture after picture after picture of when she had chosen not to hug someone.

This presence then said, "You have a choice. Either you can come, or you can go back and try again." Somewhere in her, a decision was made to come back. And she found herself waking up.

When she came back, surprisingly, she had no side effects from the pills or the liquor. She was completely alert. She knew that what she needed to do was to help people die. This was the calling.

That, to us, was so evocative. To think about what it meant to be a dying midwife, and to hear how she saw herself doing that. And also to hear her experience of what was needed to fully surrender into death. There is that need to feel like there's an integrity in our lives. It's purpose circle work. Making it good with ourselves. There's a piece of that in her story that felt really important.

ENID

Enid, our beloved landlady, was the next death. She died about ten years after we moved to Big Pine, probably in her early eighties, though she never told her age.

When we moved here, literally the day we moved here, she was just getting over a very serious illness, and in those ten years she became sick more and more often. She had a bad heart, and there were a number of times when we needed to call an ambulance to take her to the hospital. They put her into a rest home, and each time she got released they said, "You can't go home, because you have nobody to take care of you."

So we went up there and said, "We're going to steal her away. We're going to take care of her." And we brought her home.

There came a time when we brought her home again from the nursing home. She was very, very weak and couldn't really walk anymore. She said, "I want to die at home."

"Okay," we promised. "You're going to die at home."

At first we went over a couple of times a day, made her food, and cleaned her up, since she couldn't get out of bed. Derham sat with her in the evenings. Slowly it got to the point where she needed 24-hour care. For a while, Steven and I went over there at night and slept on the floor. But then our teaching season began, and we just couldn't keep doing it.

There wasn't a hospice yet in the Valley, so I called around and found people to cover different parts of the day and night. Most of the people we found to help her were Paiute women, which made her very happy. She immediately made them family.

One day, the person who was supposed to come couldn't make it. I finally found a new woman who could come for just that day. I still remember that we were meeting with a Bear Tribe group out in our backyard, and she came to the fence just as we broke up and said, "I think Enid might be dying."

She told us that all day Enid had been, saying, "Help me! Help me!" But she'd go and ask, "What do you need, Enid?" and Enid said,

"What, what?" She was obviously calling somewhere else. Because Enid didn't know this woman personally, she must have felt that she didn't need to come awake and take care of her emotionally. She seemed to have slipped into that purpose circle place, and something was happening in there.

I told the woman, "It's okay. Just keep checking on her." At the end of the day she came back again. "You've got to come," she said. We went over, and Enid had just stopped breathing. I couldn't get a heartbeat, couldn't get a pulse, so we called the mortuary.

Enid was a fighter. She should have died months before. Her death taught us that there's a way in which we die that's the same as how we live.

Enid lived the life of a single, independent woman who went on amazing adventures by herself that few other women of her time did. She went to graduate school at UC Berkeley just as the Great Depression began. She drove across the country by herself, rode mules in Baja to study her chipmunks, and was a fierce, fighting, self-reliant woman.

That's the same way she died. She fought, and it finally took being with someone she didn't know, who she didn't have to fight for or take care of, for her to do the last work of letting go.

When they came to get her body, we were in the kitchen talking about what an amazing woman she was. I just had this feeling. I quietly went into her bedroom, which was just off the kitchen. I knelt down next to her and said, "Enid! It's okay, you can go." And her bowels released. I realized that there must have been just some faint little piece of her that was still holding on, like she always did, that needed that final permission, "Enid, you can go. Just go into that vastness that you love so much."

To our utter gratitude and disbelief, she left the house to us in her will.

DERHAM

Derham's death was one of the last big teachers for me, but in a different way. He died about eight years after Steven's death. He was an amazing man and a dear, long-time friend.

It must have been four years after Steven died when I moved back to this little house of Enid's in town. Derham was still living in the room behind it. He came over one day and talked to me about having cancer. I'm the only one he told, and he didn't want other people to know. For some reason, I was the only one he really trusted.

After that, he came over now and then and we had wonderful conversations about death that went on for hours. He had no fear of death at all. Death, for him, was a mystery that intrigued him as much as the mystery of life. I loved talking with him because, in many ways, I share that curiosity. He was excited by new adventures. Still, he was afraid of dying. He was afraid of the pain.

Then one fall day I was sitting on my back step. I was just beginning my one month off from teaching when he came wandering over, looking lost. He told me that the cancer had moved into his bones. I spent that last month taking him to doctors. Our focus was on keeping him in the least pain possible and giving him the most comfort we could.

He had no family, and he wasn't close to anyone, so he didn't fear those kinds of losses when he died. I guess you'd say that I was the closest to him, but I wasn't that close. He trusted me, we were good friends, and I loved Derham, but for him, there wasn't any real attachment.   From the time we first knew Derham, he said that if he couldn't get himself up into the mountains, there was no reason to live. He wasn't being melodramatic and it wasn't a sad thing. It was just honest. His home was in the mountains. If he couldn't be there, he didn't see any reason to be alive.

Once he found out that the cancer had spread to his bones, it was amazing to watch in that last month how quickly he moved toward death. He began to lose his appetite and had a very hard time drinking water. He wasn't despondent. He just had no interest in food or water.

I spent every day with him, and we talked about wrapping up his life. We made out a simple will, entered on his computer the last data about the chipmunks in the study he had carried on after Enid died, and talked about his desire to die in the desert, which he realized would be too hard for him now.

At the end of the month, I would be flying to Europe to teach. So I began setting up some support for Derham for the time I would be gone. I introduced him to Joseph, Gigi, and Win, and I got him set up with hospice care. But these were people he didn't know, and although he appreciated what I was doing, he really didn't want to rely on them.

Looking back, I know that I was watching a man who had no attachment and no fear. In the absence of those two things, surrendering into death is quick, and pretty damn easy. It reminded me of Ginnie saying, "Wild animals know how to die. We humans have forgotten." I got the feeling I was watching an animal that instinctively knew how to die.

The pain medication I had gotten for him worked for a while, and he was able to make two more trips up into the mountains to watch the chipmunks for a couple of hours. In his little journal, his notes – he was such a scientist – he wrote, "I wonder if this is the last time I'll be coming up."

Soon he wasn't able to swallow the pills anymore. They made him sick. So toward the end of the month, I spent half a day up in Bishop trying to convince his doctor to give us some morphine. He was afraid that Derham was going to kill himself with it, which Derham probably would have done if the pain became too bad.

Earlier I had asked him, "If you really had your wish, would you want to kill yourself? Or would you rather die without that?" And his answer was, "You know, in my study of animals and insects, the more complex an organism is, the more difficult it is for me to kill it. My body has been so good to me in my life, that I wouldn't really like to kill my body. It would be hard to kill it." Which is an interesting way to see it. So I said, "Okay, we're going to do this without."

Finally his doctor gave me a very diluted version of morphine. With that, Derham would have a painkiller he could swallow more easily. When I got back home, it was the first day the hospice nurse came over, so together we went to see Derham. He couldn't get out of bed anymore, and he was no longer eating or drinking. She gave him his first dose of the morphine. It wasn't very strong, but within seconds it was clear that he was drifting in and out. It was helping him.

"Derham," I said, "I will come back every four hours through the night and give you your morphine." So every four hours, I went over and asked if he wanted more. Each time he said no, and I felt I had disturbed him.

Right before dawn, I went over again and said, "Derham, do you want some more morphine?" He said, "I want a few drops of morphine, and I want a few drops of water." So with a straw, I gave him a third of a dose of morphine and a few drops of water. He said "I'm almost there. I'm almost there," as he drifted back into some other space.

I went across the street to Joseph and asked, "Will you come and just sit with Derham while I take a quick walk? It's obviously close." When I came back an hour later, Joseph came around from behind the house and told me that Derham had just stopped breathing. I started sobbing – not from grief, but from joy for Derham. He'd figured it out. It was so beautiful that it was Joseph who was with him at the end.

Joseph said he had taken a book over and sat with him. By then Derham was in a coma. His breathing began to change. So Joseph found himself just talking to Derham and saying, "Derham, I hope you know how important you've been in the life of Meredith and Steven. And in the lives of all the people that you've touched. You've been so important to so many people. And you've helped this valley in so many ways." He just talked to him like that, and the minute he stopped talking to him, Derham stopped breathing.

It was again that sense of, not so much giving permission, but of honoring: "It's okay to go, you've done it. You've done something so big in this lifetime. It's okay to go." It just gave him that last slip. So beautiful! I felt during that month that I most likely will not have such an easy a death. I've chosen in my life to have a child, to love, and to feel deep attachment. That's going to make it harder for me to die. And that's okay, perfectly okay. I wouldn't do it any differently.

When I had cancer a couple of years ago, there was a week when I wasn't sure how much time I had left. I thought about what my path would look like to surrender to death. And I knew that it would be a path of grieving and letting go of those people I deeply love. Derham didn't have to do that. His was a different story.

RELATIONSHIP WITH MYSTERY

When I look at all these deaths, they were all so much about showing up and choosing. All of them, in the end, were about choosing. Like my father, who didn't want to go to the hospital. We were perfectly willing to overdose him on morphine, and we gave him complete control over how much he had. But he didn't want to overdose. He wanted a clear mind.

Enid, too, clearly said that she did not want to go to the hospital. She wanted to die at home. Each one offers a different learning about how to support people in their dying. It's not about trying to fix them. It's about asking, "How do I serve this person? What does she want?"

There is never one answer.

And again, it's similar to doing the rites-of-passage work, learning the skills of showing up for people and listening deeply. "This is your ceremony. It's not my ceremony." Each one taught me more about how to be there for them.

Birthing, dying, and rites of passage are the three most significant times in our lives where the sacred and profane come together as one. All three of those are incredibly profane and physical. The vision fast is lo-o-o-ng days, and it's hot, and the rocks are hard, and you get lonely – and yet, people will say it's the most sacred experience they've ever had.

This is true of birth and death as well. At a death, you feel it in the air. It's called *numinous*. One can feel the presence of something holy. It's unexplainable. You can feel that at birth, too. It's like the veil between the worlds has become very thin.

How do you serve the dying? How are you able to wash the dying, and to love their bodies, when the smell is terrible? We care for their beautiful bodies as best we can. We care for their pain as best we can. We also care for their soul, and we just love them.

This, for me, is the practice. Through all those physical deaths, I was learning how to serve people in other major life transitions. The two ceremonies fed each other. They weren't even two sides of the same coin. They were the same coin. It certainly made me more at ease with the unknown and not try to control things. It certainly taught me a lot about that. It became so clear that death is sacred, in all its forms. It is this incredible death-life. They're one thing. Not opposites.

Feeling this certainly prepared me to be more gentle with myself and my own pain when I lost Steven, which was the worst pain I've ever experienced. It would have been much more difficult for me to get through those years after Steven's death if I hadn't had the framework of a rite of passage.

This understanding made me more able to be with other people in pain, to be comfortable with people in pain. It also helped me be there for these people I loved who were dying. To know that what was happening wasn't wrong, it wasn't bad, it wasn't a failure. It was painful, yes, mostly, but it was something right that was happening.

Just like the pain of childbirth. It was so clear for me, when I gave birth to Selene, that what made the difference was that I knew, "This pain is because something good is happening." That made it different from, "Oh my God, what's wrong? Is this pain because I'm sick or I'm doing it wrong?" As hard as it is to see the labor of dying, which is very similar to the labor of birthing, it's not because something bad is happening. It's trusting that our nature knows how to do this living and dying, if we only let it, and not resist or lose that trust.

I'm so grateful for all these death teachings. I'm so grateful that I was close enough, and that I loved these people enough, to actually feel the gift that was left behind. When we allow death in, there is beauty. When Steven died, it was beautiful in the end. As much agony as there was, there was also beauty. It was like being in the room when a baby is born. That veil is so slim.

Before Steven died, I could give a pretty little story about what happens after death. But when he died, I had no idea where he went. I no longer knew where he was. Now I'm beginning to have certain stories that work for me, little bits, feeling that there is something there after our body dies. But it changes. Death continues to hone our relationship with mystery.

I think a lot of the stories we tell about what happens after death are just comfort stories. After Steven died, I asked people, "Where do you think Steven is?" I was always fascinated to hear what their story was. I got that each story said so much about the person who was living right now. There's nothing wrong with having a comfort story. But I heard some comfort stories that scared me.

I asked some people, nice people, who used to come by and knock on my door carrying their story about the Bible. They came by a little bit after Steven died, and I asked, "Okay, my husband just died. Where is he?"

The story they told was about how he was in a better place, and that there is a time when the desert will bloom with flowers, and what's happening here now on earth is unimportant. It's all about what happens after death. I began to realize how dangerous those stories are, because in many ways, they meant that people didn't have to care about what happened to the earth now. I clearly saw the danger of comfort stories that say more about our living than about our dying.

Part of the gift of having my spiritual awareness and relationship shaken over and over each time I lost someone was that it helped keep my spiritual nature curious, questioning, and growing. I feel that our relationship with our spiritual nature is something organic that needs to be revisited time and again to renew it. And it changes as I age.

I've seen, painfully, some very religious people who never questioned their religious beliefs in their lifetimes, begin to doubt as they got close to their death. Some were able to grab their faith back at the very end, and I'm glad, because it gave them comfort. But the teaching for me was how dangerous it is not to allow our spiritual curiosity to be challenged, to have our faith shaken, and to lose it and to find it again, and to lose it, and to find it again.

Because that's the way we grow. It's dangerous to try to keep it unyielding, because then, at the end, it can abandon us. I've found that supporting people at the end of their lives is also about letting them talk through their "after death" story. Hopefully, they will find one that works for them in the end.

A NEW LEGACY

A lot of these years since Steven died have been about learning the practice of "living in the moment." I realized that the only safe place for me was in the moment. It might be that the moment was full of pain, or whatever it was full of. Still, it was the only safe place. If I thought about the past, it was huge grief. If I thought about the future, it was huge despair. There was nothing I could do about either one of those.

So the only "real" place was right where I was. And I learned to stay there. Because then, at least, I could deal with the emotion. I also learned that the "yes" was to be found there.

Our doctor and friend, Scott Eberle, MD, was with us in Steven's last three months. We said to him then, "Scott, it looks like we're not going to be able to do this weaving of end-of-life and rites-of-passage program." Scott had trained at the School, and he was an experienced hospice physician. We said, "You're going to have to do it."

After Steven died, Scott asked me, "Will you do it with me?" At the time, I felt like I didn't know anything and just couldn't answer.

Then one day, when I walked in the mountains after a night of sobbing and *finally* getting it deep inside that Steven was gone, I realized that I could not do the old work that Steven and I had done together. It was just too painful, and it really was not just mine to do anymore.

What I saw as mine to do was to continue developing what we had just begun to explore together. This new work was the legacy that Steven left at the threshold of his death. I could feel a "yes" for that. It felt like a big risk to continue to teach without Steven, and taking risks somehow made me feel like I was still alive. It was a time when I could only find self-definition by what others asked of me.

Some of our people in Europe were also asking me to come back to teach, and I felt that to be a "yes" also, despite the risk and scariness. It felt like a way to continue to carry the work on for Steven, for Ginnie, for all of us. I just kept asking, "Does this feel like a yes? Does this feel like mine to do?"

But if I thought about actually being there and doing it? Huge despair and resistance. So once I said "yes" to something, I just didn't think about actually doing it. I could plan the seminar and feel the life of being creative. Yet, I could not think about doing it until I was there. When I showed up, when I sat down in that circle, then I was in the moment. I just dealt with whatever was there.

When Steven and I first began to travel to Europe to teach, we only prepared with the barest outline. We knew that when we stepped into that circle with a group of people, that together, we would go somewhere good, despite our fear. I always trusted the way we could create and feed each other and make something happen. It wasn't so much wisdom, because the essence of it was heart. Heart, empowerment, and evoking in people the discovery of their own wisdom.

Less than a year after Steven's death, a man who was a friend and who trained with us, invited Scott and me to Hawaii to do the Practice of Living and Dying seminar we had just developed. That was the first time Scott and I worked together. So it was a new partner, a first time teaching after Steven died, and a new program. A lot of risks.

But the thing that destroyed me as I sat in that circle was that all the teachings, all the understandings that I had gained in all those years working with Steven, were gone. GONE. Like ashes. They had completely vanished. I couldn't teach the Four Shields. It was not in my body anymore. It was gone. I tried to cling to remembering. My mind was trying to remember. Nothing.

Somehow, we got through it. But I was left with that terrifying feeling of having lost everything. I came home, and I pulled out all the source books, all the old anthropological books we had, and all the books that had helped us create the foundation of our work. That winter, I spent 12 hours a day going through all the old books again, and any new ones I could find, re-absorbing, re-embodying, re-discovering and finding new meaning. But this time, I was doing it as just me, and as a woman of 52 years who was not the same woman who had read them so much earlier. I was reading them as someone who had been doing this work for a long time. All winter I read, and I re-embodied the work in a new way.

For years it was frightening. I had never taught alone, and now I was doing a lot of teaching alone in Europe. Every time, I was afraid. I still didn't use notes, and I still didn't know when I sat down if anything would come out of my mouth. It was constantly shaking me – and that was okay, because it meant I was alive. I finally felt alive.

It probably took me five years before I could really say, "Okay, now I'm making footprints in the new world." I think a lot of my teaching today comes out of what I learned in those years in a very visceral way.

A lot of the work I'm passionate about today comes from the question, "How do we show up for our nature? How do we grow up, again and again, into new phases of our lives?" For me, it comes in many ways from the watching and the witnessing of myself going through this major rite of passage in my life. I really got it.

Now I can see other people doing it, and I can see phases in Steven's and my life when we did it in other ways, just not quite so dramatically. I see that theme, and I truly feel that if we have the courage to show up for what comes into our lives, to show up for all our feelings, and to learn to trust them, that our nature will move us towards healing and wholeness. That's the work I'm passionate about.

THE PRACTICE OF LIVING AND DYING

The day I was finally able to say "yes" to Scott was a turning point. And so began the creation of The Practice of Living and Dying.

I told Emerald and Joseph, who were administrators of the School at that time, "Either Scott and I can do this on our own, or we can do it through the School." I didn't really care in that moment, because I didn't really know what I cared about anymore. As always, they were their generous selves, and they supported us in creating a new arm of the School called, "The Practice of Living and Dying."

Joseph and Em didn't ask us to get permission for what we did. They just said, "Do it. We will do whatever we can to support you." How beautiful that was.

Slowly, I've found my way back into this somehow-the-same-yet-brand-new School. In addition to doing a few Practice of Living and Dying seminars, I continue to help and support the School in small – and sometimes larger – ways, like developing a new way to teach the month-long training, being part of the Elder's Council, or simply listening over dinner to Joseph or Petra sharing about what's going on in the office.

Mostly, I have tried to help seed and re-plant this work, including the Practice of Living and Dying, in new places around the world. This includes supporting our international trainees in bringing their training back to their people and culture. I feel so strongly that in our world today, which truly is a global world, we need the different international and cultural voices to mix, support, and inspire each other. And I feel the importance of this old ceremony finding its place again around the world.

The School continues to morph with the times and grow with the needs of our guides and participants. And it is a joy to be a part of the growing number of guides involved with the School who carry such integrity, individuality, commitment, and mutual respect. We continue to learn from each other, and we continue to learn from where each guide has taken the basic teachings and made them their own.

The School empowers the guides, and the guides empower and

support the people. We trust that if we empower each other, it's going to make it good for everybody. Not that there aren't shadows and bumps amidst the staff. Certainly that has happened, and there are big emotions. Yet somehow, we can encompass all that, and grow from it. Because that's what we are, and that's what we teach, and that's what this Ceremony teaches us: how to embrace everything. Not that we do it perfectly, but that we do it.

Afterword

"Yes, we are truly here. We have become a native desert plant.
We will never leave this land. Movements will rise and fall, prophets will
come and go, "what's new" will pass into history. And we'll still be growing
out here in the sandy wash beside the creek, near the boulder
dashed with spray. Come look for us."

— Steven Foster, December 6, 1996

The School is indeed still here and yes, the love story continues. This work and practice have always been intensely intimate and relational. Steven and Meredith did not make it that way, rather they were impeccable at surrendering to this truth, time and time again. This surrender to all that life brought to them, even death, shaped their lives and has become an integral aspect of our lineage.

For years we had heard them say to their trainees: "Take these teachings and ways and make them your own," and on May 6, 2003 these simple words became our mandate, as Steven's death shook us to our core. The grief was so deep and the sense of loss so pervasive — it changed us forever.

In the years that followed Steven's death, the School went through several major transitions, trying out different leadership combinations and legal forms. Within the heat of transformation, those of us who lived nearby, gathered in the form of a "guiding council:" Meredith Little, Gigi Coyle, Win Phelps, Joseph (Angelo) Lazenka, Emerald North, and Betsy Perluss. Others supported from afar: Silvia Talavera, Ruth Wharton, Larry Hobbs, John Davis, Nancy Jane, Jeffery Duval, Mary McHenry, and Scott Eberle.

Emerald and Joseph took the helm first, running the administration as a partnership. After Emerald moved to New Mexico in 2006, following the call of her entrusted muse, Joseph became sole director of the School, holding the center of the school from a single wide trailer with views of the Sierra. Without prior legal experience, bravely (or perhaps, foolishly, in the spirit of coyote) he led the way to the School becoming a non-profit, initiated by the offer of a generous donation.

As a newly established non-profit, the School faced organizational and philosophical challenges. No longer a "mom and pop," but a growing collective of dedicated, yet feral folk, including a new board of directors, things became a little more complicated. How do we, as a collective, steward the school in such a way as to not lose the essence of what makes the School unique? How do we serve our growing population of participants without getting too big? How do we ensure that our guides can continue to work freely and wildly?

Over time, the concept of interdependent autonomy emerged, which gave each guide the freedom to practice self-governance, while also taking on some measure of responsibility for the good of the whole. In the spirit of interdependent autonomy, the school operates more like an organism rather than an organization, with each guide holding certain aspects of a multi-faceted cooperative.

So who is Lost Borders today? Though we are a legal entity with forest service permits, liability insurance, fundraisers, and everything that comes with being a non-profit, at heart we are still a small band of mavericks holding onto the very same bare bones assembled at the School's beginnings. As long as Lost Borders is breathing, we will keep our work and practice simple. We are guides, not gurus. The teaching, healing and transformation comes from wild nature, solitude, ceremony, silence and the good hearts of the people who dare to venture across the threshold.

So far, it has worked. We have intentionally stayed small. We've stayed simple. Our board of directors is a council of allies helping us to navigate our way in the outer world, our elders hold the wisdom of our lineage, and our guides bring the work to their land and their people. And, we are blessed with a steady, generous core of supporters within our community that enable us to to offer scholarships and keep the ceremony accessible to all those who dare to ask.

We continue to shift in our seats, as needed, with one or two pointing the administration and tending the central fire. Most of the original core around Steven and Meredith are actively guiding even now, two decades later, profoundly and generously committed to continuing the lineage of the School. All the while, we are blessed with the steady, loving and fierce support of Meredith, founder, ally, friend and now a grandmother, offering her voice in the collective while enjoying the freedom of her independence. For her love and friendship, for always having our back, we are grateful beyond words.

At the same time, we see lots of green shoots sprouting from the rootstock: young board members have joined our tribe, some with small children, while younger guides are stepping in with new and creative visions for the work. We recognize a growing awareness and appreciation of the intersection of nature awareness, rites of passage, and social justice issues. And as Lost Borders approaches its 40th year, we bear witness to an emerging tribe of guides and partners throughout the globe. The beauty and the agony of taking a risk for what we love and asking what is ours to do in this rapidly changing world continues. May it always!

And when our bare bones finally crumble into dust, may we have partnered change well enough to inspire and sustain those who come after us. May we have grown the dream well that Steven and Meredith birthed together, and that he left in her keeping. May it have been enough. May the small imprint, the legacy we leave behind, be carved into the bedrock of existence as firmly as the fossilized spirals that live on in the gnarly washes of Death Valley, telling their story to this day, to all who dare to listen. Because love leaves a mark that simply cannot be undone.

Collaborators

Silke Schulze-Gattermann is a biographer and biography coach, a photographer of portrait and feature, and a wilderness rites-of-passage guide. See more about her work at: www.silkeschulze-gattermann.de.

Susan Hagen combines her experience as a writer and wilderness-rites-of-passage guide to offer heart-opening, life-affirming writing circles and retreats for women. See more about her work at www.susanhagen.com.

Betsy Perluss is a depth psychotherapist, ecopsychologist, and wilderness guide and trainer at the School of Lost Borders since 2002. Learn more about her work at www.psycheandnature.com and www. betsyperluss.com

Appendix

Books by Steven Foster and Meredith Little

The Book of the Vision Quest: Personal Transformation in the Wilderness
By Steven Foster and Meredith Little
First edition Island Press, 1980
Revised and expanded edition. New York: Prentice Hall, 1988

The Four Shields: The Initiatory Seasons of Human Nature
By Steven Foster with Meredith Little
Illustrated by Diagrams and drawings by James Wright; cover artist
Emerald North
Lost Borders Press, 1998

The Sacred Mountain: A Vision Fast Handbook for Adults
By Steven Foster and Meredith Little
Illustrated by Illustrations by Jennifer Massey and Carla Simmons
Lost Borders Press: Big Pine, 1996. Revised and Expanded

*Lost Borders: A Vision Fast Handbook for Youth Coming of Age
in the Wilderness*
By Steven Foster and Meredith Little
Illustrated by Illustrations by Win Bock and Jennifer Massey
Lost Borders Press: Big Pine, 1998

*The Roaring of the Sacred River: The Wilderness Quest for Vision
and Self Healing*
By Steven Foster and Meredith Little
Illustrated by Illustrations by Emerald North
Lost Borders Press: Big Pine, 1989, 1997

Bound for the Craigs of Ithaka
By Steven Foster
Lost Borders Press, 2003

We Who Have Gone Before - Memory and an Old Wilderness Midwife
By Steven Foster
Illustrated by Selene Foster
Lost Borders Press, 2002

Slide Banjo (Poetry)
By Steven Foster
Lost Borders Press, 1997

All the Way to Mulege: The Electric Alcohol Baja Bus Test
By Steven Foster
Lost Borders Press unpublished manuscript, 1975

Video by Kim Shelton

Lost Borders: Coming of Age in the Wilderness (DVD)
By Kim Shelton, Producer/Director
Two Shoes Productions. Lost Borders Press
Video – 58 minutes; DVD – 85 minutes

Books by Virginia Hine

People, Power , Change
By Virginia Hine and Luther Gerlach
Bobbs-Merrill, 1970

Lifeway Leap: The Dynamics of Change in America
By Virginia Hine and Luther Gerlach
University of Minnesota Press, 1972

"The Basic Paradigm of a Future Socio-Cultural System"
By Virginia Hine
World Issues, Volume II(2), pp. 19 - 22, 1977

Last Letter to the Pebble People
Story of her husband, Alden Hine's, dying and death
By Virginia Hine
Unity Press, 1979

Rites of Passage for Our Times: A Guide for Creating Ritual
By Virginia Hine and Steven Foster
Lost Borders Press unpublished manuscript, 1979

Self-Generated Ritual: Trend or Fad?
By Virginia Hine
Worship, Volume 55, # 5, pp. 404 – 419, 1981

Books by Enid Larson

Merriam's Chipmunk on Palo Escrito: The Life History and Naturalistic Behavior (Parts I, II, III)
By Enid A. Larson
Wacoba Press, 1981, 1986, 1987
Original notes and full manuscript at the Academy of Science,
San Francisco